CIVIL
SOCIETY

Civil Society: Historical and Contemporary Perspectives

BRIAN O'CONNELL

Civil Society: The Underpinnings of American Democracy

PHILLIP H. ROUND

By Nature and by Custom Cursed: Transatlantic Civil Discourse and New England Cultural Production, 1620–1660

Other books by Brian O'Connell

America's Voluntary Spirit (1983)

The Board Member's Book (1985)

*Board Overboard: Laughs and Lessons
For All But the Perfect Nonprofit* (1996)

Effective Leadership in Voluntary Organizations (1976)

Our Organization (1987)

People Power: Service, Advocacy, Empowerment (1994)

Philanthropy: Four Views
(with Robert Payton, Michael Novak, and Peter Dobkin Hall) (1988)

Philanthropy in Action (1987)

Powered by Coalition: The Story of INDEPENDENT SECTOR (1997)

Values (1978)

Voices from the Heart: In Celebration of America's Volunteers (1999)

Volunteers in Action (with Ann Brown O'Connell) (1989)

CIVIL SOCIETY

The Underpinnings of American Democracy

Brian O'Connell

FOREWORD BY JOHN W. GARDNER

Tufts University

Published by University Press of New England
Hanover and London

Tufts University
Published by University Press of New England, Hanover, NH 03755
© 1999 by Brian O'Connell
Printed in the United States of America
5 4 3 2
CIP data appear at the end of the book

Acknowledgments of Previously Published Material

Appreciation is extended to David Mathews and the Kettering Foundation for permission to reprint material from the Foundation's report, prepared with the assistance of the Harwood Group, "Citizens and Politics: A View from Main Street America," 1995; and material on page 107 from *Higher Education and the Practice of Democratic Politics: A Political Reader*, published by the Kettering Foundation, 1991.

Appreciation also to David Mathews for permission to reprint material on page 42 from "The Public in Practice and Theory," in *Public Administration Review*, March 1984.

Appreciation is extended to John W. Gardner for permission to reprint material on pages 51, 99, and 104–5 from *National Renewal*, a joint publication of INDEPENDENT SECTOR and National Civic League, 1995.

Appreciation is extended also to the Foundation Center for permission to reprint material on pages 45–47 and 66–70 from *Philanthropy In Action* by Brian O'Connell, 1987.

To my brothers

THOMAS E. AND JEFFREY O'CONNELL,

both academicians and authors,

who convinced me long ago

that practitioners too have an obligation

to be writers.

Contents

Foreword: The American Experiment

JOHN W. GARDNER

Think of humankind's search for social forms that honor liberty and justice and the worth and dignity of every person as a long, long story—a story that must have begun in fumbling, inarticulate ways tens of thousands of years ago. The focus here will be on the part that began some two and a half centuries ago in the British colonies on the eastern coast of North America.

The historian R. R. Palmer says that the idea of the people as the constitutive power of government was "distinctively American." The idea reached its purest expression in the Preamble to the Constitution, in the revolutionary phrase, "We, the People . . ."

In the years from 1776 through 1791 most of the fundamental principles of our society were expressed—in the Declaration of Independence, the United States Constitution, the Bill of Rights, and numerous declarations and actions by the states. The great words and phrases echo in our minds: the consent of the governed . . . equality . . . the blessings of liberty . . . the establishment of justice . . .

Those who fashioned the phrases were not unaware that they were setting high goals. In Federalist Paper 39, James Madison candidly admitted that what we were creating was "a political experiment" and that it depended "on the capacity of mankind for self-government." Thomas Jefferson too referred to it as "an experiment."

One doubts that even the most far-sighted spokesmen for the American Experiment could have envisioned the difficulties that lay ahead. After Jefferson's brave declaration that "all men are created equal" it took eighty-seven years and a bloody civil war to free the slaves, and another fifty-seven years before "We, the people," gave women the vote.

I won't list all the hard-won victories. Abraham Lincoln contributed unforgettably. Susan B. Anthony and Elizabeth Cady

Stanton sparked the nineteenth-century battle for women's rights. Samuel Gompers, an immigrant, stabilized the labor movement. In the 1930s and 1940s Thurgood Marshall and his colleagues crafted the legal victories that laid the ground for the 1954 Supreme Court decision on school desegregation, and then Martin Luther King, Jr. transformed the race issue from a legal battle to a popular movement. Betty Friedan touched off the mid-twentieth-century struggle for women's rights. La Donna Harris, Ada Deer, John Echohawk, and others put the rights of Native Americans on the agenda. Cesar Chavez gave voice and power to the Hispanic farm workers of California.

So the American Experiment is no longer simply the work of a few eighteenth-century white males. Men and women of many races and cultural origins have laid shaping hands on the American Experiment—and are still doing so. Many of those who have worked on the experiment in the past half-century think of themselves as dissidents, critics, outside the mainstream. It doesn't occur to them that they are working on the same quilt, that they have joined the large and diverse group that is still writing the long story.

Surveying the national scene today, one sees much that should put the American people in a good mood: a healthy economy, low unemployment, and so on. But they are not in a good mood. Daniel Yankelovich says there is a disconnection between the people and their leaders. The polls show that they do not trust government.

Another troubling aspect is the loss of any sense of the future. When most of us were growing up, we took a bright future for granted. In those times, for Americans all over the nation, the future was the repository of expectations and dreams—not just for ourselves but for humankind. Our minds were alive with possibility and hope.

Americans have reason for negative attitudes today. But the sad, hard truth is that at this juncture the American people themselves are a part of the problem. Cynicism, alienation, and disaffection do not move problems toward solution. We need a powerful thrust of energy to move this nation through a rough patch, and *much of that energy will have to come from the citizens themselves.*

We can best gird ourselves for the path ahead by reigniting some of the seminal, explosive ideas of the past: the ideas I've already listed and others—an open climate for dissent, inalienable-rights, and not least the old, great, American idea of getting people off other people's backs—a concept we are still working on after all these years.

The American Experiment is still in the laboratory. And there could be no nobler task for our generation than to move that great effort along.

One might imagine that the straightforward path to repair the civic faith of Americans would be to make government worthy of their faith. But the plain truth is that government (and other powerful institutions) will not become worthy of trust until citizens take positive action to hold them to account.

Citizen involvement comes first. And a fortunate by-product is that when citizens become involved their morale improves. I cannot emphasize too strongly that a prime ingredient in the citizen's negative mood is a sense of disconnection. "We, the People" feel a long way from the centers of decision. It doesn't seem like our venture any more. Anything that repairs the sense of connection will help repair the mood.

In the past several years the most publicized form of citizen involvement has been community service—volunteers at work in one or another area of social improvement. Such service has been so popularized that it is seen by some as the beginning and end of the citizen's responsibility. In truth, it is only one way to discharge that responsibility—but it is very important.

Advocacy is equally important. Voting is of course the most basic form and low voter turnout is distressing. But advocacy should extend far beyond the voting booth. Our national parks, the pure food and drug laws, and the vote for women are testimony that successful citizen advocacy is well rooted in our history. Government needs the goading and support that citizens supply. More and more citizens are learning how to organize to do battle with the powerful entrenched interests with which they often collide. Tough-minded politicians know that citizens can make a difference.

There are extraordinary things happening at the grass roots today, in city after city across this nation—so extraordinary that I believe we are beginning to write a whole new chapter in the tumultuous American story.

Who would have believed that Cleveland would make a spectacular comeback after heartbreaking years of racial, political, and financial troubles, which climaxed when their polluted river caught fire. Cleveland still has far to go but the turnaround is remarkable. Who would have believed that sleepy Chattanooga would decide in the mid-1980s that it wanted to be the best midsized city in the nation by the year 2000—and that it would then achieve civic goals that surprised us all? Who would have predicted that tradition-laden Charlotte, North Carolina, would emerge as one of the nation's most powerful banking centers and at the same time develop enlightened patterns of neighborhood development?

In most cities, there is a striving toward new patterns of collaboration—new partnerships—among government agencies (at all levels) and the private sector, for-profit and nonprofit. Everyone recognizes that municipal government working alone cannot save the city. Collaboration is crucial.

What we need is a reasonable balance between the claims of individuality and the claims of community. Community involves constraints. We argue about the constraints and revise them periodically, but we cannot do without them.

A requirement essential to contemporary community building is that we bring into being a wholeness that incorporates diversity. This requires that we enable diverse groups to know one another. It requires techniques of conflict resolution, coalition building, and collaborative problem solving. It requires institutions that transcend group differences. Racism and the growing gap between rich and poor pose grave difficulties. The achievement of wholeness that incorporates diversity is the transcendent task for our generation, at home and worldwide.

A great civilization is a drama lived in the minds of a people. It is a shared vision, shared norms, expectations, and values. In today's climate, many Americans are so put off by the zealots in our national conversation that they are reluctant even to talk about values. But every successful society we know anything about has created a framework of law, unwritten customs, norms of conduct, and values to channel human behavior toward purposes it deems acceptable. Social commentators have an understandable impulse to focus on our disagreements over values. But if we care about the American Experiment we had better search out and celebrate the values we share.

Societies that keep their values alive do so not by escaping the process of decay but by powerful processes of regeneration. That we have failed and fumbled in some of our attempts to achieve our ideals is obvious. But the great ideas still beckon—freedom, equality, justice, the release of human possibilities. And we have an uncelebrated capacity to counter disintegration with new integrations.

If the values we profess are paramount, how should we behave? It isn't enough to talk about respect for human dignity. What does it imply for employment and housing policy? It isn't enough to talk about individual fulfillment. What does it imply for action in education and health? How should our institutions be designed? How should our government behave? What changes are called for in the real world? What can we do to help bring those changes about?

It requires great insight and understanding to draw strength from the past, to search out the truths that it offers, to learn its lessons, however bitter, to face present challenges, however uncomfortable, and to honor our profound obligation to the future.

So those who have not succumbed to the contemporary disaffection and alienation must speak the word of life to their fellow Americans. It is not a liberal or conservative issue. It is not Democrat versus Republican. It is a question of whether we are going to settle into a permanent state of alienated self-absorption or show the vigor and purpose that becomes us. We do not want it said that after a couple of great centuries we let the American Experiment disintegrate.

When the American spirit awakens it transforms worlds. But it does not awaken without a challenge. Citizens need to understand that this moment in history does in fact present a challenge that demands the best that is in them.

Can they come to understand that? I direct your attention to a trait shared by a great many citizens of this land. There is in them something waiting to be awakened, wanting to be awakened. Most Americans welcome the voice that lifts them out of themselves. They want to be better people. They want to help make this a better country.

You do not need to tell them that the nation is in trouble, or that humanity is in trouble. They know that. What you can do is to awaken them to the possibilities within themselves. Awaken them to what *they* can do for their country, the country of their children and their children's children.

We are capable of so much more than is now asked of us. The courage and spirit are there, poorly hidden beneath our surface

pragmatism and self-indulgence, left somnolent by the moral indifference of modern life, waiting to be called forth when the moment comes.

I'm saying that the moment has come. And of the voices you
will want to listen to, I can't think of any more relevant than Brian
O'Connell's.

Preface

Civil Society: The Underpinnings of American Democracy attempts to respond to growing interest in the subject of civil society and growing confusion about what civil society is and does. The book reflects my belief that civil society is essential to American democracy, but so little is understood about it that democracy is undermined.

I began thinking about this project and organizing materials for it about six years ago, but at that point I was still president of INDE-PENDENT SECTOR with limited time to devote to the effort. Even after stepping out of an active role there, I had continuing obligations, including writing the history of INDEPENDENT SECTOR, getting involved with the Filene Center at Tufts, and helping sort out and explain the consequences of devolution and reinventing government, particularly for local government and voluntary organizations.

During this period the interest in and confusion about civil society were escalating; at least five national commissions on the subject were operating and hundreds of studies had begun.

There was also corresponding growth in the literature on civil society, though the differences of opinion expressed, including definitions and examples, tended to add to the confusion of those struggling to figure out what the excitement and even the subject were all about.

Schools and colleges and leaders in the independent sector and public administration were rapidly increasing their attention to such subjects as effective governance, civics, service learning, pluralism, voluntary action, and philanthropy. Interest in the subject escalated also around the world, and most of those trying to strengthen or even establish their own civil societies were turning to this country for their most prominent example.

By 1997 it was clear that if I were ever to undertake such a volume, I had to seize the moment.

The book is designed to provide insights and examples of the concept and practice of civil society. I come at the topic with keen awareness of the need to be clear and to target the topic for the practical understanding and action of community and national leaders, including mayors, civic leaders, school boards, public administrators, independent sector leaders, scholars, and teachers.

My orientation and experience derive from almost half a century as a community organizer with a career focus on citizen service and influence. Though almost all of that activity has been within the United States, I served also as head of the organizing committee and as first chair for CIVICUS: World Alliance for Citizen Participation, and as chair of an early Salzburg Seminar on international comparisons of voluntary/philanthropic activity.

Throughout my career as an organizer, I've tried to keep reasonably abreast of the literature, with recent emphasis on civil society. In that regard, the book acknowledges the scholarly works and reflects my admiration of them without losing my focus as a practitioner. I have tried to remain riveted to my role as an organizer, including trying to be candid where I think the scholars miss key points or fail to communicate them. For example, most scholars define civil society as the space *between* government and the individual, overlooking the key role that government plays in preserving such essential elements as freedom of speech and right of association, and the role that individuals fulfill as the basic unit of democratic government. Also, few writers even mention the roles of business and free enterprise as pivotal factors in the development and effectiveness of our civil society.

The book is not a treatise on the subject. My focus at every stage has been to produce a small practical book that represents a ground-level view of the underpinnings of our democracy, which might spark greater attention to a subject so basic to liberated people and societies.

Among my intended audiences are those we used to call "public intellectuals," those citizens who read, think, and converse about the large public issues of their times and are prepared to act on them. I believe wholeheartedly in the public role and capacity of the citizenry at large, but I also believe it's important to target that special and large group of leaders, whether scholars, legislators, merchants, or tradespeople, who should be encouraged to embrace again or at least more intently, a focus on the public good. Many of the leaders of our communities and nation are concerned about how citizens can reengage themselves and expand their influence on society including government. They want to make government more effective and achieve the fuller functioning of democracy, but they are confused about what is really wrong and what they can do to help. They are the "public intellectuals" I want very much to reach.

Finally, the book does not attempt to be dispassionate. I hope it is passionate without being shrill and a call to action without preaching.

Many people have helped with what for me was a particularly complex task and without whom the book would not have been possible.

Sharon Stewart at INDEPENDENT SECTOR assisted at the earliest stage of collecting and organizing resource materials. Her role and a great deal more were later transferred to Sandi Gasbarro at the Filene Center, who has been extraordinarily capable and patient throughout the process of putting it all together. Also at the Center, Rob Hollister and Badi Foster, successive directors, have been supportive and encouraging. At the university level, President John DiBiaggio and John Schneider, our representative to the University Press of New England, were central to initiating the Tufts Civil Society Series at the press and encouraging me to be part of its launching. At the University Press, the various people who have expedited the project have been enthusiastic and helpful—a welcome combination.

Mara O'Connell Duke, graphics artist and designer, helped me figure out how to portray civil society and deserves credit for the illustrations that appear in chapter 2. Adam Yarmolinsky helped me understand and describe Constitutional and other legal considerations that have influenced the establishment and development of our civil society and democracy. Virginia Hodgkinson's conversations and writings aided greatly in the presentation and translation of important statistics and other data.

The funders of my professorship at Tufts, including time to concentrate on the book, deserve special credit. They are the

Ford and Kellogg foundations and an anonymous donor. The Packard Foundation was helpful in covering extra expenses related to the book.

I had not thought to impose on John Gardner for involvement with this additional project, but when I read his piece, "The American Experiment," delivered initially to the Council for Excellence in Government at the National Press Club, I felt it was so absolutely right for use here, I asked him to consider adapting it as the Foreword. I am delighted and grateful for his agreement and the result.

This project overlapped substantially with the book *Voices From the Heart: In Celebration of America's Volunteers*, which was published almost simultaneously. It was not sensible to pursue them in tandem, but the opportunities to do two things I felt so deeply about came along at just about the same time and neither could be postponed. I mention this to underscore the depth of my acknowledgment of Ann B. O'Connell's personal and professional support during more than two years of these preoccupations, especially at a time in our lives when she had reason to expect better. The books and I couldn't have come out of the experience intact without her forbearance, steady disposition, and substantial participation.

October 1998   B.O'C.

CIVIL
SOCIETY

1

Civil Society—
Our Invisible Colossus

This notion of community is one of the most charac-
teristic, one of the most important, yet one of the least
noticed American contributions to modern life.
DANIEL AND RUTH BOORSTIN in *Hidden History*

I was twenty-three years old before I began to understand that
there was anything like what we now call civil society, or even that
there was all around me such a thing as a voluntary, nonprofit, independent sector.

I was born in a nonprofit hospital, raised in a Catholic family,
have been a Boy Scout, member of the YMCA, active in the Junior
Red Cross, and raised money for the March of Dimes. I helped organize a student chapter of United World Federalists, gained initial appreciation of the arts at our local museum, loved watching
my father on stage at the Players' Club, attended a private college,
worked six months at a private school clinic for handicapped children, and had hundreds of other exposures to citizen participation
and influence without thinking much about them.

I had particularly liked courses in American history, government, and civics, was a student delegate in a process to study and
reorganize our city's form of government, had volunteered and
served two years in the U.S. Army, observed a presidential con-
vention, was fascinated that the people overwhelmed the pun-
dits in Truman's victory over Dewey, decided on a career in city

management, and was well into a graduate program in public administration before it dawned on me that there was something in
our way of life—something vast and vital—that somehow I had
missed in all that education and experience, but to which I was
being drawn.

I hadn't realized that there was a sprawling and deeply layered
web of voluntary associations and institutions, that religions did
more than preach their gospels, that people are often ahead of
their leaders, and that democracy really rests on the underpinnings of citizen participation and influence. I thought it was all
much simpler—the Constitution, three branches of government,
political parties and elections, foreign policy, assistance to the
needy, a free press, and free enterprise. Keep them operating and
America rumbled on.

The defining experience for me in understanding what it takes
to keep it all rumbling, and even all together, was simple, profound, and slow to penetrate. It related to that six-month assign-
ment with the disability clinic I mentioned before.

After graduating from Tufts in early 1953 and with six months
to go before graduate school, I needed to earn some money and
hoped I could find something that would give me experience in
public work. The closest short-term opportunity was a staff job in
an association devoted to what today we call developmental disabilities such as cerebral palsy. The association was comprised primarily of parents who shared a fierce belief in the potential of
their children and a bond forged by pervasive professional advice
to put their sorry children away and get on with their own lives.
Their relatively new school clinic was struggling to keep open and
to provide at least minimal physical therapy and education for
about twenty youngsters. As great as the pressure was simply to
maintain the operation, it was outmatched by the uproar from the
scores of families on the waiting list and by everyone's insistence
that the services had to be increased.

Many of the kids and parents were not particularly appealing to
this sheltered newcomer. Some of the little ones were often wildly
spastic, with more spittle than speech, and some of the parents
were so used to fighting and rejection that they were alternately
raging in your face and sobbing on your shoulder. The parents
were determined that their kids could and would learn and talk
and get around. The forces that drove them were not necessarily

guilt or blind hope, though there was plenty of both. They knew from daily and hourly attendance on their kids that there was much more within them than professionals saw, and they would not rest until it was coaxed out.

By the time I got there, the association—largely the parents—had convinced the county to lend them a closed wing in a very old and dilapidated hospital, hired a physical therapist to train the parents to work with their children, and convinced the school board and superintendent to assign two public school teachers to work full time with these ragged pupils in a gradually promising effort to test and nurture their learning potential.

Though the operation was still tiny and terribly fragile, what was evolving began to serve as a model and to provide hope and courage for struggling parents and enlightened professionals in communities throughout the country.

During my brief stay, we—again mostly the parents—raised enough money to maintain and slightly enlarge the program for a year, extended the physical therapy training to many on the waiting list, stabilized somewhat an association made chaotic by the desperation of the parents, and began to get better media coverage, usually around the "miracle" of such kids walking and reading.

With that fascinating interlude behind me, I was off to Syracuse and the Maxwell School of Citizenship and Public Affairs to prepare for "real" public service. This experience started positively, but I found I couldn't quite shake thoughts of my school clinic and my increasing examination of it as significant public work. Gradually, I realized I was becoming committed to these prior activities, which represented positive public results and public process, and that I wasn't going to learn more about them in even a very good school of public administration.

I recall the reactions of some of the faculty when I announced I would be leaving. My recent bride was now pregnant, and though we might have found a way to do without her salary, our revised circumstances hastened my decision to pursue the different track of what I almost alone on the campus seemed to recognize as public endeavor. Fortunately I had been invited back to the association and school clinic in the newly created post of executive director.

When I explained the plan to my faculty advisor, he told me

with every good intention that I would be a real loss to public life. I was too surprised to express adequately a different view of my fate, but I was pretty sure then, and know for certain now, that public service should be more broadly defined and that such schools should provide broader orientation about how the public's business is conducted and what constitutes public service.

I retained my interest in and respect for public administration, and in later years have worked to achieve a broader understanding of what *public* really means, including in public administration and service. Though I am still viewed somewhat as a stranger, it's an indication of progress that in the 1980s I was elected a Fellow of the National Academy of Public Administration and now serve on its board.

From those beginnings as a community organizer, my focus has been on citizen service and influence, which, along with my involvement in public administration, led me to a natural interest in the concept and practice of civil society, including the many intersections of the governmental and independent sectors.

In that regard, I should acknowledge that my example of the wonderfully effective advocates in the school clinic is far from encompassing the whole of civil society or even the voluntary sector. It is used up front because it represented for me the defining experience of the essentiality of citizen participation and influence and because it is inclusive of some of what I've learned are essential characteristics of free and effective societies, such as:

1. Civic space where citizens with similar interests and concerns can find one another and are free to pursue what they believe is in their and the public's interest.
2. Freedom of speech, including criticism of those in power.
3. The right of association and the exercise of collective action.
4. Citizen impact on public policies and programs and on public attitudes and behavior.
5. Effective and responsive government, especially officials who respect that citizens are the beginning point of *public* and that citizen influence and participation are essential to effective public policies and programs.

To provide another view of this elusive giant called civil society, I want to leap ahead for a moment to the early nineties and an experience that helped illuminate for me what after forty years I was still struggling to understand.

In 1991 Jim Joseph, who was then head of the Council on Foundations, and I, as president of INDEPENDENT SECTOR, were asked to determine how and even *if* foundations and others in the United States should respond to burgeoning requests from people around the world for help in strengthening citizen initiative in their countries.

To assist in this endeavor, we assembled twenty-seven people from twenty-three countries, diverse political settings, and widely varied experiences with our subject. We did the recruiting job almost too well: we were all the way into our second meeting without achieving agreement on descriptions and terms. In our terribly disparate group, there were entirely different interpretations and reactions to such words and practices as philanthropy, voluntarism, civic and civil society, pluralism, nonprofit or nongovernmental organizations, advocacy, empowerment, participatory government, and on and on.

At a point when we might have concluded that people who couldn't figure out what they had in common had little chance to decide what to do about it, one of our members, Miklós Marschall, then deputy mayor of Budapest and a leader of the so-called "informals" of predemocratic Hungary, observed that it was unlikely we could ever agree on terms that meant such different things in our various languages and cultures, but that what he was hearing around the table suggested that we all seemed to agree that effective societies exist in direct proportion to their degree of citizen participation and influence. With that articulation, our divided, quarrelsome, and wary group suddenly found common ground, and with a shared sense of purpose and urgency, moved rapidly to create what has become CIVICUS: World Alliance for Citizen Participation. We concluded our report:

> Most of us had not met when we became involved in this consideration, and most of us were skeptical at the very least that anything could be accomplished. We have moved from the condition of unallied doubters to a unified body embracing a shared vision. Despite all of our differences and differentness, we are agreed that something very significant may be unfolding in the world and that the moment should be seized.[1]

I learned through that experience that there is a universal and unquenchable hunger for participation and influence within one's own surroundings and in matters affecting one's own destiny, and that it is absolutely stifling when there is only the one governmental system for providing work, food, education, health care, religion, and so many other basic human needs and aspirations.

I also understood better how much the rest of the world recognizes and envies our advanced state of what they often describe as buffer zones between government and the individual. Far better than ourselves, they realize what we've got and how absolutely essential it is to liberation. They know too that though democracies are much more likely to encourage and allow independent citizen initiative, achieving a democratic form of government does not by itself ensure support for such essentials as freedom of speech and right of association.

The key messages for me in this experience were how truly fortunate we are to have a buffer—participatory, independent, influential civil society; how much more clearly our blessings are understood outside the country than within; and how fragile these rights and opportunities are even in democracies.

As I review those two personal experiences, one at midcentury and the other at century's close, I have to acknowledge that what had been invisible to me so long ago is still largely indistinct to most people in the United States, including the leaders who have the greatest influence on public policies and attitudes. Though we have made progress, it is alarmingly clear that we have not come very far in achieving a real grasp of civil society's profound significance. Civil society and even the web of omnipresent voluntary organizations remain obscure, as do the relevance of them to what we cherish as the American experience. Unfortunately, our situation can still be summarized by Jefferson's words on the Liberty Pole at Union Square in New York: "How little my countrymen know what precious blessings they are in possession of and which no other people on earth enjoy."

Recent changes in eastern and central Europe provide some greater awareness of how very fortunate Americans are and of the dangers of taking our good fortune for granted. In *Conditions of Liberty*, Ernest Gellner traces the transitions in Europe and their relevance for us, including dealing with the factor of invisibility. In his chapter "Civil Society and Its Rivals," he notes:

> Atlantic society is endowed with Civil Society, and on the whole, at any rate since 1945, it has enjoyed it without giving it much or any thought. . . . It is only the rediscovery of this ideal in Eastern Europe in the course of the last two decades that has reminded the inhabitants of the liberal states on either shore of the northern Atlantic of just what it is that they possess and ought to hold dear. . . . [The collapse of Marxism] has taught us how better to understand the American experience, the nature of our previously half-felt, half-understood values.[2]

At about the same time that CIVICUS was being formed, Vaclav Havel, president of the Czech Republic, captured the importance of this growing worldwide interest in citizen participation when he said, "The modern era is at its height, and if we are not to perish of our modernness we have to rehabilitate the human dimension of citizenship."[3]

I'm constantly struck by the contradiction between how much our opportunities, even our freedoms, depend on the quality of our civil life, and how little we understand or invest in it. There is the occasional Fourth of July celebration to remind us of the blessings of freedom, but we don't seem to be aware that these essential underpinnings of democracy were created for all Americans and passed on to us for safekeeping.

Unfortunately, we generally prefer to rely on structures such as representative government and the courts, to maintain the marvels of American democracy, but even they deteriorate without the devotion and investment of their citizen masters. The ultimate preservation rests upon the forceful awareness of the populace that ultimately our social fabric, our democratic government, and our freedom depend on us. As the great jurist Learned Hand expressed it:

> I often wonder whether we do not rest our hopes too much upon constitutions, upon laws and courts. These are false hopes; believe me, these are false hopes. Liberty lies in the hearts of men; when it dies there, no constitution, no law, no court can save it.[4]

Thomas Jefferson took the factor of awareness to the critical next
level of personal commitment:

> Where every man is . . . participator in the government of affairs,
> not merely at an election one day in the year but every day . . . he
> will let the heart be torn out of his body sooner than his power be
> wrested from him by a Caesar or a Bonapart.[5]

Public Policy and Citizenship, edited by Helen Ingram and Stephen
Rathgeb Smith for the Brookings Institution, points out that our
duties are often far less dramatic than combat but still absolutely
necessary:

> Few may be asked to fight in battle, but all will be given an oppor-
> tunity to sacrifice private pleasures for some public purpose. To do
> so, one must have the capacity to care about the common good as
> well as confidence in one's ability to help attain it.[6]

At the very time there is so much worldwide attention to civic
engagement and so much interest in this country about civil society, there is a contradictory debate swirling in higher education
about whether schools and universities should teach citizenship
and civil society. Some don't think the subject scholarly enough.
When that disturbing notion was surfacing in the 1980s, I was invited to give the keynote address at the American Association of
Higher Education's national conference, and I took the opportunity to say:

> The United States is the longest-lived democracy in the history of
> the world. This democracy has provided almost all of us with
> greater freedom and opportunity than any nation of human beings
> has ever known. Among the crucial factors that foster and preserve
> that democracy and those freedoms are active citizenship and per-
> sonal community service. No leader or leadership institution—par-
> ticularly no educator or educational institution—can presume that
> fostering active citizenship to prolong our democracy and to ex-
> tend those glorious freedoms for those who come after us is some-
> one else's business.[7]

In *Philanthropy: Voluntary Action for the Public Good*, Robert L.
Payton warns of the consequences of failing to understand and

undergird these essential attributes of democracy. Speaking of philanthropy literally as "love of mankind," he concludes that "the new *Encyclopedia Britannica* overlooks philanthropy, as far as I can tell, although an earlier edition—the eleventh—dealt with it quite adequately. That's the way it goes: One day you take it for granted, and the next day it's gone."[8]

A necessary step toward visibility and understanding, which are the essential prerequisites for personal commitment and vigilance, involves a riveting grasp of what civil society is and specifically what is expected of each of us. I know from frequent failures to communicate these matters that we've got to find better words and ways to penetrate the ideas and ideals involved. An effort to do that begins with definitions and descriptions in the next chapter.

2

Definitions and Descriptions

Those who expect to reap the blessings of freedom
must undergo the fatigue of supporting it.
THOMAS PAINE, 1777

Any hope of achieving awareness of civil society depends on our
ability to make it strikingly visible and manifestly consequential.
That begins with a solid understanding of just what civil society is
and does.

Providing a crisp definition is compounded by major differences in the way scholars view civil society. Benjamin Barber says,
"The more the term civil society has been used in recent years, the
less it has been understood."[1]

To try to make the message as clear as possible I'm going to be
fairly definite about what I believe civil society is, based on almost
half a century of immersion in it and at least reasonable acquain-
tance with the literature, including recognition of some common
ground among scholars. My boldness is based on the need to interpret and reinforce these shared perceptions before acknowledging,
in later chapters, the inevitable nuances and differences of opinion.

I find that clarity on the topic has to start with correcting two
common misperceptions: that civil society is synonymous with the
voluntary, independent sector, and that civil society is synonymous with civility. Civil society includes both the independent
sector and civility but also a great deal more.

The most common agreement about civil society is that it represents the balance between the rights granted to individuals in

free societies and the responsibilities required of citizens to maintain those rights.

I am reminded constantly of the searching for common ground among the worldwide organizers of CIVICUS and our realization that it is a common truth for our times that small, everyday freedoms and the liberty of societies depend on the degree to which citizens are allowed to have influence and do in fact exercise that power. Conversely, that experience made me all the more aware that to be denied or to lose those everyday rights is to be trapped in suffocating powerlessness.

That fact that most people agree on the literal balance between rights and responsibilities was brought home to me by the surprising similarity of views of the radical Saul Alinsky and the arch conservative William F. Buckley, Jr. For example, Alinsky says in *Rules for Radicals*:

> People cannot be free unless they are willing to sacrifice some of their interests to guarantee the freedom of others. . . . Citizen participation is the animating spirit and force in a society predicated on voluntarism.[2]

In *Gratitude: Reflections on What We Owe to Our Country*, Buckley says:

> The conservative movement perceives connections between the individual and the community beyond those that relate either to the state or to the marketplace. . . .
>
> It was this essentially conservative insight that the liberal John Stuart Mill expressed when he wrote that "though society is not founded on a contract . . . everyone who receives the protection of society owes a return for the benefit, and the fact of living in a society renders it indispensable that each should be bound to observe a certain line of conduct toward the rest."[3]

To convince most citizens of this need to be involved, it is essential to make obvious the freedoms that are worth fighting for. Without trying to be exhaustive, I will indicate some of those rights and privileges with which we are blessed and without which it would be our generation's obligation to become America's revolutionaries.

1. A democracy where the people are ultimately in charge.
2. Representative government, starting with one person/one vote.
3. Freedom of religion, speech, and assembly.
4. Respect and protection for most of what we do in our private lives.
5. Protection of our safety and property.
6. The right to exercise personal initiative to deal with the problems and needs of our communities.
7. The right of association.
8. A system of justice beginning with due process and presumption of innocence.
9. Free press.
10. Universal public education.
11. Free enterprise.
12. Social security and other public support programs.

To keep the balance, here is a list of some of our responsibilities:

1. Participation in government, beginning with the realization that citizens are the primary unit of government and that, unless we vote, speak out, and take part in the process and structure of government, democracy and therefore our freedoms are undermined.
2. Personal service to people through our acts of neighborliness and compassion, and through building the informal structures and networks that undergird communities and democracy.
3. Participation and support for the causes of our choice that help retain and build our traditions of organized neighborliness and private initiative for the public good.
4. Civility in our dealings with others, including those we don't know.
5. Vigilance in protecting freedoms and rights for ourselves and others.
6. Obedience to the law.
7. Payment of taxes.
8. Willingness to defend the country.

For a part of society that is so fundamental, it is curious that few of us could describe the place from which civil society operates and exercises such sweeping influence. Though my overall goal in the book is to simplify the topic, I have to admit that on the matter of location and parameters, simple answers lead to even greater confusion or inadequate understatement. For example, the most common description is that civil society occupies the space *between* government and the individual, or the space not occupied by government or commerce. But, these descriptions fail to indicate adequately the primary role of citizens within government and the roles of government in setting forth and preserving the freedoms. Those descriptions also fail to acknowledge the public services and the public problem solving roles of business.

Sara M. Evans and Harry C. Boyte, in *Free Spaces: The Sources of Democratic Change in America*, locate the primary territory of civil society as "The public spaces, in which ordinary people become participants in the complex, ambiguous, engaging conversation about democracy: participators in governance rather than spectators or complainers, victims or accomplices."[4] They elaborate:

> The central argument of this book is that particular sorts of public places in the community, what we call free spaces, are the environments in which people are able to learn a new self-respect, a deeper and more assertive group identity, public skills, and values of cooperation and civic virtue.[5]

Even with these very helpful indicators it's still a struggle to describe and place civil society in a way that causes students and leaders to respond, "I'm finally *really* getting it." After repeated failures at communicating the "it," I believe I'm at least getting closer to what and where I've learned civil society to be. Acknowledging all the complexity, let me try to provide a manageable description.

The Individual

Civil society begins with self, the individual, and our private lives. Too many descriptions, though acknowledging the balance between rights and obligations, leap into the duties before being sure that an individual *really* understands the enormous personal benefits derived from a healthy civil society. Though there is cooperation and generosity in almost all of us, there is also a lot of self-interest. We need to acknowledge it before we can move to the levels of collective self-interest and altruism.

In *Gift From the Sea*, Ann Morrow Lindbergh makes the case that it's essential and certainly not selfish to attend to one's own core.

> When we start at the center of ourselves, we discover something worthwhile extending toward the periphery of the circle (family, significant others, etc.). We find again some of the joy in the now, some of the peace in the here, some of the love in me and thee which go to make up the kingdom of heaven on earth.[6]

To diagram it, civil society starts with the INDIVIDUAL, represented by the inner core—the circle.

Some characteristics of the individual:

- Self
- My Private Life
- My Space
- My Beliefs
- Family
- Friends
- Expectation of Respect and Civility from Others
- Enlightened Self-Interest, Which Leads to Collective Consideration and Action

The Community

From our private lives I move to COMMUNITY, where almost every element of our private lives depends on the quality of our immediate surroundings—including neighborhoods, congregations, associations, clubs, parks, museums, hospitals, and local government—and where the quality of those interconnections depends on collective obligation and performance.

Not everything in community is civil society per se but to the extent that communities produce basic services, amenities, organized neighborliness, and civility, most of what communities are and do nurtures and protects the individual, provides opportunities for human development, and teaches us about our interdependence. In his essay "Building Community," Gardner points out:

> Families and communities are the ground-level generators and preservers of values and ethical systems. No society can remain vital or even survive without a reasonable base of shared values—and such values are not established by edict from lofty levels of society. They are generated chiefly in the family, school, church, and other intimate settings in which people deal with one another face to face.[7]

Community is also where civility becomes an essential aspect of interrelationships and behavior, and therefore this is probably the best place to define it. Civility, in the dictionary definition, is "politeness, kindness, consideration, and courtesy."[8] It is the "golden rule to do unto others as you would have them do unto you." It is to behave as a fellow citizen sharing space, rights, and responsibilities, and reflecting mutual dependence on one another for the quality and preservation of our individual and collective rights. In sum, it is to be civilized.

COMMUNITY intersects with almost every other aspect of our personal lives.

Some features of community that relate distinctly to civil society:

- Neighbors
- Congregations
- Associations
- Clubs
- Recreation
- Work
- Arts
- Hospitals
- Local Government
- Civility

Government

GOVERNMENT is the third component of civil society. It's an element often left out in definitions of civil society, which focus only on the space that exists *between* the individual and government. It's my view that any definition of civil society in the United States has to include the essential participation of citizens in democratic government and the essential role of government in providing and protecting citizen participation in the first place. Most of what government does is not central to civil society—for example, the military, foreign policy, and interstate commerce—but even those functions are ultimately related to freedom and opportunity.

GOVERNMENT depends on citizenship and provides such freedoms as speech and assembly so necessary to the existence and quality of civil society.

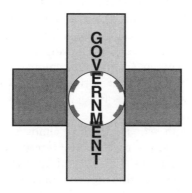

Some aspects of government that provide personal liberation and require personal responsibility:

- Citizenship
- Freedom
- Rights
- Courts
- Security
- Education
- Voting
- Participating in Political Parties
- Obeying Laws
- Paying Taxes
- Civility

Business

The BUSINESS sector is another undervalued partner in civil society. Many businesses are not renowned for civility and social conscience, but those that accept and fulfill social responsibility contribute significantly to the quality of community and civil society. I've often seen what a positive role corporations and their leaders play in bettering their surroundings. A large proportion of voluntary organizations and their fundraising campaigns are led by businessmen and women. Companies, unions, and media contribute greatly to the well-being of institutions and associations, and a company that is a good corporate citizen is concerned about its people and community.

Even Adam Smith, who is identified almost singularly with private enterprise, made the case for the interdependence of commerce and civil society. In "On Moral Imperatives," James A. Joseph puts Smith's views in this broader context.

> Smith is remembered best for what he had to say about economics, but he was a moral philosopher, not an economist. He wrote *A Theory of Moral Sentiments* before he wrote *The Wealth of Nations*. His economic theories were based on his ideas about moral community, especially the notion that the individual has the moral duty to have regard for fellow human beings.[9]

One's place of work and the relationship between company and consumer must also represent civility if there is to be quality of life and long-term commercial success.

What businesses do that directly relates to civil society is a smaller percentage of their total activity than that of government and community, but the contributions business makes and their significance are still enormous.

BUSINESS is part of America's civil society.

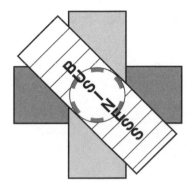

Some features of business that contribute to civil society:

- Free Enterprise
- Jobs
- Marketplace and Freedom of Choice
- Media to Involve and Connect Us
- Professional Societies
- Unions
- Social Responsibility
- Corporate Philanthropy
- Employee Public Service
- Civility

Voluntary Participation

The VOLUNTARY, nonprofit, independent sector is central to the definition and function of civil society. At times this sector of activity is even mistakenly considered to be all of civil society.

Not everything that occurs in the nonprofit realm is necessarily a part of civil society, and certainly some charities are identified more with self-interest than public benefit, but most of the country's vast charitable endeavor is very much part of civil society.

VOLUNTARY participation and the independent sector.

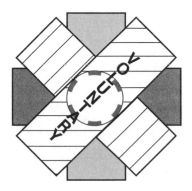

Some features of the independent sector that relate to civil society:

- Volunteers
- Associations
- Religion
- Private Colleges, Museums, etc.
- Clubs
- Foundations
- School and Hospital Boards, etc.
- Crusades and Crusaders
- Self Help or Mutual Assistance Groups
- Political Parties
- Civility

Civil society exists at the intersection where the various elements of society come together to protect and nurture the individual and where the individual operates to provide those same protections and liberating opportunities for others.

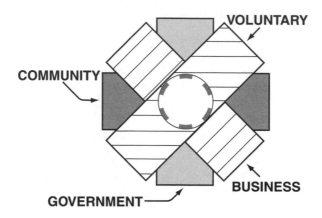

Civil society might be symbolized by the star that results from putting all these sectors and forces into common perspective. The rays are the influence of citizens on every part of society, and citizens are the common focus of all elements of society.

The important mix of all the players in civil society and their influence on each other are becoming more visible thanks to those scholars who compare the overall health of various communities and countries. In the article "The Prosperous Community," from *Making Democracy Work*, a study of the relative health of different regions of Italy, Robert Putnam writes that "Civic was a major influence, not just on the social fabric, but also on the quality of government and commerce." He concludes:

> They [the healthy communities] have become rich because they were civic. The social capital embodied in norms and networks of civic engagement seems to be a precondition for economic development, as well as for effective government. Development economists take note: Civics matters.[10]

The symbiosis of all these parts of our own civil society produces an extra dimension that is even greater than the sum of the parts.

Before I move on, there is one other fairly basic definitional matter to cover, concerning the relationship between democracy and civil society, including which comes first and is the more important. In some quarters, particularly in Europe, the two are increasingly referred to interchangeably. Though I agree that civil society is necessary to democracy, I do not believe it is a synonym for it. My experience is that the order of importance is democracy and then civil society, with full awareness that a vibrant civil society is most likely to thrive in a vibrant democracy and vice versa. Civil society exists in nondemocratic countries, it is growing in size and importance in Saudi Arabia, for example, and there are democracies where civil society is weak, as in Japan. The central point is that a healthy, vibrant civil society is both the fullest indication of and a precondition for a healthy democracy.

In the United States we need to be particularly careful not to confuse a public already comfortable with and proud of our democracy. We shouldn't do anything that takes our eyes off its glory and the need to maintain and strengthen it. Therefore, I emphasize the idea that civil society is absolutely necessary to a fully functioning democracy and democracy is the ultimate form of government of, by, and for the people.

The importance of our civil society to our democracy is indeed a secret of our success as a nation, but the very fact that it is so little understood means that it is always in danger of neglect and attack, and with any significant alteration or diminution of civil society, our freedoms are similarly weakened.

Our secret may become better known and appreciated if we realize just how these rights and privileges came to be established and passed along to us. The next chapter traces some of the origins and evolution of these rights with the hope that we will become more conscious of our sacred obligation to pass along not just the rights but the awareness of the civic roles and skills necessary to preserve them for future generations.

3

Origins of Our
Extraordinary Civil Society

And for the support of this Declaration . . . we mutually pledge to each other our Lives, our Fortunes and
our sacred Honor.

DECLARATION OF INDEPENDENCE

Obviously, ours is not the only civil society in the world. Civil society exists everywhere, but nowhere are its proportions and influence so great as in the United States. If we believe that these patterns and levels of participation contribute essentially to American
life, we need to understand and nurture all of the roots that give
rise to such glorious degrees of personal liberation and national
freedom.

How it started and developed is not easy to sort out. This is an
aspect of our national life we have taken for granted and never
really felt much of a need to study. Lately however, as concerns
have arisen here about the quality of our civic and social fabric and
as people from other countries have shown increasing interest in
how they might learn from our example, there has been a scramble to understand what we've got and how we achieved it. Without
pretending to be a historian, I will indicate some factors I've come
to identify as preconditions for a healthy civil society—what Gellner describes as "conditions of liberty."

From my own experience and reading, these conditions are

many and complicated, and attempts to simplify them have often clouded our understanding. For example, the most prevalent explanation is that our civil society derives from our Protestant ethic and English ancestry, but my own experience and a growing body of literature suggest that as important as that ethic and ancestry are, they are only two of many significant sources. What we identify as "Christian" or even "Judeo-Christian" impulses were also brought to our shores by each wave of immigrants, whether they came from Sweden, Africa, China, or India, and whether they followed Jesus, Moses, Mohammed, or Buddha.[1]

I've learned too that we shouldn't even assume that these characteristics and traditions were imported. In "Doing Good in the New World" from his *American Philanthropy*, historian Robert Bremner makes clear that the Indians treated us with far more Christian goodness than we practiced on them. Reading his descriptions of the kindly way in which most Indians greeted intruders and helped them adjust to their world, one is absolutely wrenched out of prior notions about imported goodness.[2]

Though the English are too often given more than their share of credit, we shouldn't undervalue the early and significant influences of the Puritans, pilgrims, and English law. From the law, we drew our basic concepts of rights, due process, and other essential protections of persons and property. Even though our Declaration of Independence, Constitution, and earlier documents such as the Federalist Papers helped sever our English ties, they reflected a great many positive elements of English heritage.

One of the most significant writings of the earliest English settlers came from John Winthrop, the first governor of Massachusetts. He wrote it just before he and his fellow Puritans boarded the *Arbella* to come to America in 1630, and read it aloud for the first time during the voyage. "A Model of Christian Charity" was intended to help the group understand how they would have to behave toward one another to survive and make the most of their opportunities in the New World. For example:

> We must be knit together in this work as one man; we must enter-
> tain each other in brotherly affection; —we must uphold a familiar
> commerce together in all meekness, gentleness, patience and liber-
> ality. We must delight in each other, make other's conditions our
> own, rejoice together, mourn together, labor and suffer together;

always having before our eyes our commission and community as members of the same body.[3]

As important as religious influences have been, we can't ascribe our traditions solely to their lessons of goodness. Matters of pure need and mutual dependence and assistance can't be overlooked. The Minutemen and frontier families practiced basic forms of enlightened self-interest. To portray our history of participation as relating solely to goodness may describe the best of our forebears, but it ignores the widespread tradition of organized neighborliness that hardship dictated and goodness tempered.

We came into a country where there was very little structure; we had a chance to start all over again. For most people, for the first time in generations, the family hierarchy was absent. There were few built-in restraints imposed by centuries of laws and habits, and yet we were terribly interdependent. In the absence of families and controlling traditions, we addressed our dependence and gregariousness by becoming, as Max Lerner described it, "a nation of joiners."[4] These new institutions, whether they were churches, unions, granges, fire companies, or other specific organizations, became our networks for socializing and mutual activity.

It's also important to realize that we were people determined never again to be ruled by kings or emperors or czars and thus were suspicious of any central authority. We were resolved that power should be spread. This meant, for example, that voluntary institutions carried a large share of what governments did in other countries. In an INDEPENDENT SECTOR piece, "What Kind of Society Shall We Have?" Richard W. Lyman, former president of the Rockefeller Foundation and president emeritus of Stanford University, reminds us of Burke's description of "the little platoons" of France that became our own way of achieving dispersion of power and organization of mutual effort.[5]

As we experienced the benefits of so much citizen participation, including the personal satisfactions that such involvement provides, we became all the more committed to this kind of participatory society. Along the way, we constantly renewed our faith in the basic intelligence and ability of people. We have never found a better substitute for safeguarding freedom than placing responsibility in the hands of the people and expecting them to fulfill it. We can be disappointed at times in their performance, but the ultimate answer is still the democratic compact. We can be discouraged with the complexity of today's issues and concerned that the people won't make the right decisions for themselves, their families, and their communities, but there is wisdom and comfort still in Thomas Jefferson's advice:

> I know of no safe depository of the ultimate powers of society, but the people themselves; and if we think them not enlightened enough to exercise their control with a wholesome discretion, the remedy is not to take it from them, but to inform their discretion by education.[6]

We really meant and continue to mean what is written in the Declaration of Independence. We do believe in the rights and powers of people, and these convictions cause us to stand up and be counted on a broad array of issues, and to cherish and fiercely defend the freedoms of religion, speech, and assembly. The later Bill of Rights reinforced our freedoms and constituted another reminder to people here and abroad that a great deal of struggle was necessary to secure our liberty and rights. In 1990, on the two hundredth anniversary of that document, Lech Walesa observed:

> I'm not sure the American people have any idea how blessed they are to have the Bill of Rights.
>
> After all, who needs a document to guarantee rights that people already presume they have? Ask the people who tore down fences and jumped walls. Ask the people who were cut off from their families and deprived of their jobs. Ask my fellow workers at the Gdansk shipyard.
>
> Freedom may be the soul of humanity, but sometimes you have to struggle to prove it.[7]

The Bill of Rights really became a living document only well into our second century. Indeed, it's been primarily since the end of World War II that the United States Supreme Court gave its provisions fullest meaning in ways that have supported a truly inclusive civil society. The Court achieved this through school desegregation in the Brown case, through protection of the rights of the accused poor and powerless (from the famous Miranda warnings to the provision of counsel to those who cannot afford it), and through the protection of unpopular speech and writing, in a long series of cases.

These judicial decisions have been supplemented by legislative and executive actions aimed at achieving a more inclusive society: amendments to the Constitution such as that providing women's suffrage, and legislation such as the Civil Rights Act, the Americans with Disabilities Act, and the Social Security Act.[8]

Not to be overlooked are the routine but fundamental court protections of freedoms of speech, assembly, association, and religion. The very routineness of them are an absolute glory of the American way, too often taken for granted but deeply envied throughout the world.

We also owe a great deal to the organizations that have been doggedly dedicated to those freedoms, such as American Civil Liberties Union (ACLU), National Conference of Christians and Jews, the Southern Christian Leadership Conference, the Anti-Defamation League, the American Friends Service Committee, Amnesty International, and the National Organization of Women (NOW).

The importance of legal underpinnings is highlighted in a document prepared for people attempting to establish or strengthen civil society in their countries. In the opening chapter of "Legal Principles for Citizen Participation: Toward a Legal Framework for Civil Society Organizations" CIVICUS emphasizes that "Law alone cannot create a society that is open to citizen participation, but no open society can exist unless the law gives meaningful protection to those rights that are fundamental to freedom, such as the freedoms of expression, association, and peaceful assembly."[9]

The nation's early and continuing commitment to pluralism and pluralistic problem solving has also provided a significant precondition of our civil society. In *Care and Community in Modern Society*, Virginia Hodgkinson, Paul G. Schervish, and Margaret Gates summarize recent research on factors relating to this country's pluralism:

> The United States is a pluralistic nation made up of citizens that originally emigrated from most of the other nations in the world. Leaving countries where a single ethnic or racial group made up the majority of the culture also meant leaving many institutional forms of caring and participating, ranging from extended families,

tribes or guilds to nationally supported religious institutions or even government structures designed to serve homogeneous groups. In the United States, structural arrangements to bring disparate people into association with one another to conduct their public business have led to a predominance of institutions and cultural mores different both in number and in influence from those in other countries where the citizenry is not ethnically and racially diverse.[10]

The social economist Estelle James, now at the World Bank, has been conducting important and fascinating research to determine why pluralism and other aspects of civil society thrive or don't thrive in different countries and cultures. From her study of more than a dozen countries, James believes that the presence of four critical factors is the primary determinant of strong civil behavior.

1. There are many different religions, including a variety of local congregations providing independent religious expression and opportunities for small groups to come together regularly to exchange ideas.
2. The people of wealth are not the same as those who control the government, which means that they tend to establish associations, colleges, museums, and other institutions independent of government.
3. The population is heterogeneous, including many different ethnic backgrounds, so the people are likely to look at things from different perspectives.
4. The country and government are decentralized and pluralistic, spreading responsibility among levels of government and between government, businesses, and nonprofit organizations.

Obviously, all four positive preconditions are present in abundance in the United States. Conversely, there are decided limits on civic behavior if:

1. There is only one state or primary religion.
2. The people of wealth are also the people in control of government.
3. The population is primarily homogeneous, for example, all with similar ancestry.

4. The country is centralized, with the central government pretty much the primary player.[11]

In William M. Sullivan's "The Infrastructure of Democracy," a somewhat different but supporting profile emerges from the work relating to Putnam's Italy studies:

> In his landmark study of Italian regional governments, Robert Putnam developed a set of characteristics, as well as empirical measures, of the kind of social space necessary for "making democracy work. . . ."
>
> The first characteristic of successful regions was civic engagement, the expectation that individuals and groups are "alive to the interests of others."
>
> The second was a high degree of political equality, defined as a social context in which "horizontal relationships of reciprocity and cooperation" predominate over "vertical relationships of authority and dependence." . . .
>
> Thirdly, civic regions were characterized by high levels of solidarity, trust, and tolerance. This enabled citizens to cooperate with different others for the sake of developing public goods.
>
> Fourth, civic regions were places of dense and overlapping associational life. This developed the skills of cooperation and habits of shared responsibility.[12]

In "Mediating Structures" from the book *Voluntary Associations*, James Luther Adams emphasizes separation of powers and decentralization of authority as essential to healthy societies:

> For Madison, the separation of powers is the touchstone of a democratic society. Only through this division can freedom be achieved or preserved. Separation should therefore appear at the different levels in society, from the federal government to the various mediating structures in the public as well as in the private sector. Madison favored a government powerful enough to preserve order, an order balanced by a society with liberty enough to prevent tyranny. The major "desideratum," he says is order and freedom.[13]

In an address to INDEPENDENT SECTOR's 1987 conference on "The Constitution and the Independent Sector," David Mathews

pointed out the independent sector's role in spreading responsibility and participation, for example "the role of the sector in bring-
ing together people formally and informally, to deal with shared
issues makes it the most 'public' of the sectors in the context of
'public life' as our shared life in all its forms."[14]

Though much of our civil society was born in the founding years
and in early documents such as the Declaration of Independence
and Constitution, what has evolved is even more participatory and
democratic than the founders intended. Historian Peter Dobkin
Hall points out that the early expectations were that the elite
would continue as leaders, and that the pluralism that exists today
was never envisioned. However, in keeping with Estelle James's
finding that voluntary institutions abound within heterogeneous
populations and where the people of wealth are not necessarily
those who control government, Hall suggests that the United
States became more populist and far more dependent on voluntary institutions to carry out public business than had been antici-
pated. In "Public Policy: A Historical Appraisal," Hall writes:

> Not surprisingly, the groups most acutely aware of the conse-
> quences of democracy in America were those who lost the most by
> it. Those who had once commanded deference by virtue of office
> (ministers) or lineage (old colonial dynasties) or wealth (merchants)
> suddenly found that these counted for little in the scramble for
> fame, fortune, and political office that emerged with the new cen-
> tury. . . . At the same time, they recognized that political disenfran-
> chisement did not entirely deprive them of opportunities for influ-
> ence: the abstention of constitutional government from moral and
> perceptual agenda-making, combined with the capacity to freely
> form voluntary associations, made it possible for minorities like
> themselves to devote themselves to the production of knowledge,
> the propagation of values, and the training of leadership.[15]

A great fear in our early years and still echoing 250 years later is
that control by the masses might result in chaos and greed with
everyone looking out for themselves and no one looking out for
the commonweal. However, Jefferson's faith in the people (and
subsequent laws such as those that protect us from the tyranny of

the majority or minority) are reflected in 1995 findings, reported in *Voice and Equality* by Sidney Verba, Kay Lehman Schlozman, and Henry E. Brady.

> In a fuller participatory democracy, political activity becomes a mechanism whereby citizens engage in enlightened discourse, come to understand the views of others, and become sensitized to the needs of the community and nation. Thus educated, they transcend their own interests to seek the public good. . . . In discussing the reasons they become active, participants make clear to an extent we found surprising—that they think of themselves as acting for the common good. This does not mean that they do not also use their participation as a vehicle for furthering their own narrow interests or, to make the analytical task more complicated, that they do not sometimes construe what is good for themselves as being good for the country. Still, in a cynical era in which self-interested rhetoric is the norm, we were impressed with the level of respondents' concern for the common good and the extent to which they believed their activity to be motivated by it.[16]

For those who assumed that such wholesale participation would lead inevitably to socialism, Adam B. Seligman in *The Idea of Civil Society* examines why America held to democracy even in the face of "the socialist movement as it grew and developed in different European societies in the nineteenth and twentieth centuries [and which] represented more than anything else, an attempt to broaden the basis of membership and participation in society."[17]

After examining several differences between the American and European experiences, Seligman sums up:

> From a comparative perspective it thus becomes clear that a full understanding of the failure of socialism in the United States is to be found not in any set of structural factors or political constraints *per se*, but in the overriding terms of American ideology, with its inclusive definitions of citizenship and its integration of the working class as members of the national collective. More than anything else it was the very ideology of Americanism, *its civil religion*, in Bellah's terms, that precluded the development of a socialist movement here.[18]

About midway through our life as a nation, Alexis de Tocqueville took stock of what had developed. In "Of the Uses Which Americans Make of Public Associations" from his *Democracy in America*, Tocqueville provided these often quoted observations:

> Nothing, in my opinion, is more deserving of our attention than the intellectual and moral associations of America. The political and industrial associations of that country strike us forcibly; but the others elude our observation, or if we discover them, we understand them imperfectly because we have hardly ever seen anything of the kind. It must be acknowledged, however, that they are as necessary to the American people as the former, and perhaps more so. In democratic countries the science of associations is the mother science; the progress of all the rest depends upon the progress it has made.
>
> Among the laws that rule human societies there is one which seems to be more precise and clear than all others. If men are to remain civilized or to become so, the art of associating together must grow and improve in the same ratio in which the quality of conditions is increased.[19]

Almost 150 years later, in 1982, Richard Reeves retraced Tocqueville's travels and wrote about it in *American Journey*. Reeves' principal observation is that "Tocqueville had it right" and that a century and a half later "Tocqueville's observations are still on target," with the patterns of participation strong and growing.[20]

In "Thomas Jefferson, Equality and the Creation of a Civil Society," Gordon S. Wood ties together the origins of equality and cooperation and the eventual development of our civil society. Early in his paper Wood says, "Common ordinary Americans have more of this feeling of social equality than most other peoples, and Thomas Jefferson and the American Revolution were crucial in creating it."[21] Wood ends by saying:

> And all the while equality was what made this civil society work. It became the central force of the culture and the source of modern associational life. Americans became the ultimate contract-making people, held together not by traditional tribal blood or hierarchical dependency but by the modern trust that came from treating everyone, even strangers, as equal individuals. This modern trust

among equal individuals may not run deep, may not compare to the tribal ties for which men will die, and may not create the kind of romantic communities that some of us yearn for; but it is enough for a functioning, prosperous, democratic civil society. And it is the kind of trust that depends on a belief in the equality of all the participants, a belief in equality for which Jefferson has been the supreme spokesman.[22]

Jean Bethke Elshtain gives another contemporary viewpoint in *Democracy on Trial.*

[America] means that one can share a dream of political possibility, which is to say, a dream of democracy; it means that one can make one's voice heard; it means both individual accomplishment as well as a sense of responsibility; it means sharing the possibility of a brotherhood and sisterhood that is perhaps fractious—as all brotherhoods and sisterhoods are—and yet united in a spirit that's a spirit more of good than ill will; it means that one is marked by history but not totally burdened with it and defined by it; it means that one can expect some basic sense of fair play.[23]

I can't end this chapter on origins without correcting one misunderstanding that crops up repeatedly when people here and abroad try to provide a simplistic explanation for our vast independent sector. Over and over again, otherwise interested and well-informed individuals say something like: "Well of course our tax code and its allowance of tax deductions for charitable contributions accounts for our extraordinary generosity and our vast voluntary network." Actually, only about 20 percent of us itemize our tax returns, usually the financially well off, so 80 percent don't use the tax deduction at all. Also, the great majority of contributions come from those with average or below-average incomes, and low income families are more likely to be generous with what they've got than the well-to-do.

Even among the wealthy, the tax deduction is not a factor in why people give. All studies on the topic indicate that people contribute for the right reasons—they want to help others and communities and causes. The availability of the tax deduction *does* increase the *size* of their contributions on the order of approximately 30 percent. That's an important factor of support but not the primary one.

Though I have tried to stay largely with the United States experience, I readily acknowledge that the origins of our civil society can be traced back to the very earliest awareness of human coexistence. Our notion of what constitutes healthy and liberating societies comes from many quarters, including the lessons of early religions and civilizations, the examples of places like Rome, Athens, and Sparta, and the writings of early scholars and observers such as Aristotle, Plato, Pericles, Kant, Hobbes, Hume, Locke, Ferguson, Hegel, and Paine.

They have provided an almost dizzying variety of philosophies and terminologies, such as democratic socialist, social democrat, classical republicanism, and civic humanism, with differing emphases on the responsibilities of government and individuals. But the common message is that free and effective people require all the liberating elements of good government and good government requires all the responsible participation of good citizens.

4

Effective Citizenship → Effective Government → Effective Citizenship

> We think about how dependent the public is on good
> government . . . but we lose sight of how much good
> government needs a good public.
>
> DAVID MATHEWS

I mentioned earlier that all my experience suggests that any definition of civil society in the United States has to include the essential participation of citizens in democratic government and the essential role of government in providing and protecting citizen
participation in the first place.

In *Civitas: A Framework for Civic Education*, the authors trace to
Aristotle in 340 B.C. the belief that citizens are the basic unit of
democratic government: "If liberty and equality, as is thought by
some, are chiefly to be found in democracy, they will be attained
when all persons alike share in the government to the utmost."[1]
There was also the Athenian Code, which stated: "We will ever
strive for the ideals and sacred things of the city, both alone and
with many: we will unceasingly seek to quicken the sense of public
duty: we will transmit this city not less, but greater, better and
more beautiful that it was transmitted to us."[2]

With hindsight, Edward Gibbon was able to diagnose why the
Athenians did not remain loyal to that noble purpose:

In the end, more than they wanted freedom, they wanted security. They wanted a comfortable life and they lost it all—security, comfort and freedom. . . . When the Athenians finally wanted not to give to society but for society to give to them, when the freedom they wished for most was freedom from responsibility, then Athens ceased to be free.[3]

Almost everyone's list of citizen obligations begins with voting. In other parts of the book I'll deal with the sorry state of voting in America, but for now I will note what Theodore Roosevelt observed about the consequences of failing to fulfill such ordinary duties: "You cannot expect the highest type of citizenship in the periods when it is needed most if that citizenship has not been trained by faithful performance of ordinary duty."[4]

Involvement in elections and politics are characteristics of effective citizens; and the more citizens remove themselves from politics, the less chance we have of making our democracy better. Many people today are doubtful and even cynical about the effectiveness and responsiveness of their elected officials, but here too the solution is to use and improve the system, not to give up on it.

Michael Pertschuk in *Giant Killers* provides encouragement about the ability of citizens to have influence. He says, "Citizen movements—and especially the coupling of those movements with the craft of political advocacy—can make Washington and other legislatures respond and topple giant private interests."[5] In *The Quickening of America: Rebuilding Our Nation, Remaking Our Lives*, Frances Moore Lappé and Paul Martin DuBois provide scores of examples of ways in which citizens are increasing their influence in their neighborhoods and communities. In the chapter "Governing 'By the People,' " they describe one coalition's ability to lift the minimum wage:

The minimum wage is the lowest hourly wage an employer can legally offer. Somewhere, some government body must set it. To Grace Trejo, a Los Angeles homemaker and first-generation American, raising the minimum wage appeared far beyond reach. In just nine months in 1987, however, Grace and other low-to-moderate-income Americans in three citizen organizations—affiliates of the Industrial Areas Foundation in Southern California—

launched the Moral Minimum Wage campaign and conquered what she called "a mountain."

"Whole families were falling apart," she reported, because of the stress caused by low wages. So Grace and other regular Americans in the IAF network did research to uncover just who decides the minimum wage. In California, the answer is the Industrial Welfare Commission—just five people. Grace and her cohorts then *personalized* the impersonal, distant power of the commission. They actively educated Muriel Morse, the commission's swing vote. They took her into their homes to show her the impact of low wages on families.

In the end, with five hundred citizens crowding the hearing room, the commission voted three to two to increase the minimum wage by 27 percent. Grace remembered how she felt that day: "We really did it! That's a moment you never want to forget." And soon the federal government followed California's lead.[6]

This power of ordinary people is emphasized throughout *The Rebirth of Urban Democracy* by Jeffrey M. Berry, Kent Portney, and Ken Thomson. In their chapter "Participatory Democracy, Representative Democracy," they recount the growing presence and importance of neighborhood associations, which "give people of all income levels more control over decisions that affect the quality of life in their communities."[7]

Along with citizens' fulfilling their responsibilities to make government effective, civil society depends on government to protect and foster active citizenship and private initiative. On that score, there was a good news/bad news quality to a recent article by Eugene W. Hickok of the Civil Society Project. In "Federalism, Citizenship and Community" Hickok writes about "the declining quality of American democracy," but points to many signs and examples of "restoration of citizenship and community." He concludes by calling for "reform that is guided by the proposition that what matters is not how much power and influence the government has but how much power and influence the citizens have and how government can help citizens exercise that power and influence."[8]

Many of Hickok's examples reflect the contradiction between government's unease in dealing with citizens yet realizing that such involvement is the key to cooperation and results. In my own frequent experience, people in government decry the lack of public support for their efforts—such as support of bond issues—but they want that support at arm's length without the tension of significant involvement. I don't suggest that people who work for government are generally antagonistic to citizens and their organizations, but there is certainly a great deal of ambivalence that frequently crosses the line to antipathy. David Mathews in a *Public Administration Review* article, "The Public in Practice and Theory," reflected on his own experience as secretary of Health, Education and Welfare. After careful examination of the obstacles to the "availability" and the consequences of the "unavailability" of citizen participation, Mathews observes:

> The way government operated in relation to the people and to democratic precepts was disquieting. It was not that bureaucrats were "bad" people whose values differ from ours. It was not that the government was in the hands of bunglers. The problem went deeper. It had to do with what happened to the public in public administration. The public was, for the most part, unavailable.
>
> For some officials and bureaucrats, the public was unavailable because it was an abstraction. The abstraction was to be honored in principle, to be recognized rhetorically, but in practice, the real public was not essential in the operation of government. The view was that ours was a representative democracy; therefore it was not necessary to deal with the public directly in ways other than through elections.
>
> It follows that if the quality of the public, or the public life, is not good, or not as good as it could be, then the quality of the things that depend upon it are in jeopardy. . . . There can be no vital political life, no viable institutions of government, no sense of mastery over our shared fate, no effective common endeavors of any kind without there being a foundation of public awareness and spirit.[9]

A rather strange experience I had will indicate the very large gap between acknowledging the need for citizen involvement and achieving it. I was approached by a management consultant who was under contract with a government in the Middle East that needed to establish a new community far into the desert. Oil had been struck and required a great many people to extract it, which meant that workers and their families had to be persuaded to move to the desolate spot. Someone got the notion that if the government could offer the attractions of a community complete with all imaginable support systems and amenities, the task might be doable.

What the consultant wanted me to do was to enumerate the support systems and amenities of an ideal American community, and then advise them how to set these up, with everything paid for and sustained by the government. I explained that a very real part of the attraction of such entities in the United States is that the people really own and feel responsible for these associations and systems and want a good deal to say about how they are operated. I indicated that if all these community activities and organizations were owned and controlled by the government, they would not have at all the qualities the government was seeking. It took only a short time for the message to come back that the government could not and would not tolerate such independent people and in-stitutions and that therefore they would have to find a different way to accomplish their purposes.

While that experience borders on absurd, it nevertheless sticks in my mind as symbolic of how many places in the world, and even in the United States, there is a great desire to have active citizens as long as people and their organizations know their places and don't make waves.

In a paper "Can Philanthropy Solve the Problems of Civil Soci-ety," prepared for the International Conference on Civil Society, Bruce Sievers of the international organization Synergos pointed out how difficult it is to establish a true civil society in totalitarian and other statist regimes:

> Civil societies' problems thus can be seen to take different forms in different societies. In totalitarian systems there is absent indepen-dent associational life which can only be supplied by the civil struc-tures that the system itself eradicates. Ironically, it is only these structures that can supply the legitimacy and genuine commitment to the polity which regimes so desperately seek to create.[10]

In "To Empower People: The Role of Mediating Structures in Public Policy," Peter L. Berger and Richard John Neuhaus

identify and describe four critical mediating structures: neighborhood, family, church, and voluntary associations. They then make
three particular points about such institutions: "Mediating structures are essential. . . . Public policy should protect mediating
structures. . . . Public policy should utilize mediating institutions."[11] They conclude that empowerment of people and populations is the key to effective societies and that it is in the interest of
government to find every possible way to achieve empowerment
as a basic tenet of enlightened governance.

Amid current concerns about quality of government in the United
States and therefore about the quality of our citizenship, there is a
general call for a whole new look at how government operates,
and a desire to bring citizens more to the fore. In a paraphrase of
Georges Clemenceau's "war is too important to be left to the gen-
erals," people are suggesting that government is too important to
be left to the professionals. There is, for example, increasing interest in recreating the state and community citizen leagues that were
part of what was referred to as the "good government movement"
of the early 1900s.
    In the current scramble to deal with "reinventing government,"
"devolution," "privatization," and other such reorganization
schemes, more and more communities are looking to citizen leaders to help sort out what changes need to be made and how. One
of the best of these is the Local Investment Commission (LINC),
which operates in Kansas City and many other parts of Missouri
where government officials have given citizen leaders considerable sway in studying and proposing major changes in the way
government services are organized and financed.
    Taking a look at one sphere in which citizen participation is
common, David Mathews asks, "Is There a Public for Public
Schools?"

> The public is slipping away from the public schools, and no one
> seems to be paying much attention. If the relationship between cit-
> izens and what are supposedly *their* schools is weak, fragile, and in
> disrepair, the first thing we need to do is not weaken it further. If
> the supports for a bridge have deteriorated, you don't keep driving
> eighteen-wheelers over it.[12]

"Is there a public?" could be asked just as easily about the public and health or environment or any other important aspect of community and national life.

Daniel Boorstin echoes this call for greater citizen involvement and leadership in "Democracy's Secret Virtue," in which he puts forward the view that "to protect democracy we need to enliven the amateur spirit."

> The amateur spirit is a distinctive virtue of democracy. Every year, as professions and bureaucracies increase in power, it becomes more difficult—yet more urgent—to keep that spirit alive. . . . Only leaders informed by this amateur spirit can prepare us for the one certainty in history—which is the unexpected.[13]

The World Bank and other international aid groups are learning that their best investments are often those that build capacity for citizen voice and impact. In "The State, Popular Participation, and the Voluntary Sector," John Clark of the World Bank pays particular attention to the role of nongovernmental organizations (NGOs) in expanding civil society; that role, he argues, is frequently more important than specific support for housing, food distribution, and so on.[14]

In preparing *Philanthropy in Action*,[15] Ann B. O'Connell and I searched for grants by individuals, foundations, and corporations that had made a seminal difference in areas critical to society. In the course of it we came across a number of funders and grants, generally in the early 1900s, designed to increase the participation of citizen leaders in government. In the chapter "To Preserve and Enhance Democratic Government and Institutions," we focused on the unique contributions of funders of good government. We found that both the Citizens Union, created in 1897, and the New York Bureau of Municipal Research, created in 1904, were established in response to concerns about corrupt and inefficient city government, starting in New York City. A few courageous individuals had finally decided to confront the corruption and power of the likes of Tammany Hall. Their objectives were simply stated, but almost impossible to fulfill: they wanted to create citizen interest, involvement, and control in the exercise of democratic government; to attract able people into government service; and to study how to achieve effective and responsible governance. The bosses and clubs that exercised iron-fisted control of municipal government in almost all major cities vigorously resisted such efforts.

The New York success story is told by Luther Gulick in the *National Institute of Public Administration: A Progress Report*[16] and by Jane S. Dahlberg in the *New York Bureau of Municipal Research: Pioneer in Government Administration*.[17] The two give appropriate credit to many, but clearly assign primary credit to three people: a civic leader, a professional administrator, and a generous and steadfast donor. The civic leader was R. Fulton Cutting, the founding chairman of the Bureau, who also headed the Citizens' Union where the Bureau started. The professional was Dr. William H. Allan, author of *Efficient Democracy*, and the philanthropist was Mary (Mrs. E. H.) Harriman.

Much later, when the Bureau sought to establish a training school for public service, Harriman donated the necessary money. Dahlberg writes:

> Mrs. Harriman, whose husband had been one of the early supporters of the New York Bureau, maintained contact with the Bureau after her husband's death in 1910. She returned from a visit late in 1910, enthusiastic about the caliber of men in the British Government's Career Service. She thought that more young men from families of influence in this country should enter public life. She offered to contribute money to Harvard, Yale or Columbia for training of such men for government service, but was scornfully turned down as politics was considered dirty at worst and non-academic at best.[18]

Harriman instead gave the money to establish what became the New York Training School for Public Service, the prototype for schools of public service that thereafter began to spring up across the country. The New York school's training activities were later taken on by another philanthropist, George H. Maxwell, who, according Dahlberg, "wished to donate money for citizenship training." The Maxwell School of Citizenship and Public Affairs, providing for graduate education and preparation for government service, was moved to Syracuse University and is still one of the most respected institutions in this field.

This story has a later ironic twist. As with many fields, disciplines, and professions, public administration has now become so professionalized that some of its leaders worry that it is leaving behind responsiveness to the notions of citizen participation and responsibility that were its initial inspiration. A noted Maxwell School faculty member, Frederick C. Mosher, pointed up the dilemma with his observation that "Participation by private citizens runs a collision course with professionalism."[19] With full acknowledgment of that tension, another distinguished public administrator and teacher, Ralph R. Widner, says that "we must rearrange the relationship between citizens and public administrators":

> Citizens are likely to remain angry and cynical and distrustful, and will continue to drop-out from elections, unless we re-arrange the connection between them and their governments.
>
> Yes governments must be more clearly accountable for their decisions and their actions.
>
> But most of the truly messy domestic problems we face today cannot be resolved by governments *at any level* unless citizens themselves are more accountable, responsible, and engaged in helping to solve them.[20]

Widner concludes that "the public administrator must relinquish his or her accustomed professional command-and-control role in favor of the role of facilitator and support. With leadership by public administrators, this is happening in hundreds of communities, a development scarcely recognized in national deliberations."[21]

As someone interested in both the independent and governmental sectors, who has watched the increasing role of business corporations in the delivery of public services, I find that even good schools of public administration fail to provide their students with a broad understanding of how the public business is done or even of the roles of citizens in keeping government effective and responsive.

Sometimes when I speak to groups, particularly those composed primarily of government leaders, I find that many interpret my words to mean that public administrators and politicians should bow to the whim of every shouting citizen. On the contrary, I advocate strong politicians and administrative leaders who are sufficiently confident and capable to know how important it is to be attuned to citizens *without* having to accommodate every shrill voice. Good government leaders learn to listen for citizen concerns and suggestions while looking behind each proposal to see if it is logical and if it affects enough people to merit consideration. I find that today's able leaders have a capacity for controversy and an ability to know when adjustment is necessary or unnecessary.

More than a decade ago I was asked to give the keynote address at the NOW Legal Defense and Education Fund's Tenth Anniversary Convocation on the subject of "Future Leadership in America."[22] The message I tried to get across, and still do, is that it is important to our national morale and essential to our perspective that we recognize and rejoice in the fact that Americans have enormous influence on their lives, their communities, their country, and their world.

It is important to realize that such active participation and leadership are now evident in every segment of our society. Our dilemma is not a dearth of leadership, but a natural delay in developing leaders capable of understanding and capitalizing on the staggering multiplication of participants and the dizzying dispersion of power.

At one extreme, we have many well-meaning people who are so bewildered by the explosion of the power structure into every corner of the community and country that, in order to solve problems, they want to get that power structure back into a manageable system where a smaller group is again in charge. At the other extreme are those who believe that the lessons of the sixties and seventies have taught us how essential it is that people have greater control of their own destinies. Whether it's expressed as doing one's own thing or empowerment, we are all now rigidly alert to the value and joy of having options and alternatives, and of having the power of citizens to influence our surroundings.

In essence, we have been painfully relearning the fundamental lesson of our ancestors, that freedom is the preeminent value. That lesson has come so hard for many of us that we are suspicious and wary of any interconnections that in any way might detract from our independence. Along the way, we have become skeptical, bordering on cynical, about most of our institutions, even those created to serve or unite us. We want democratic government to serve the common need but are frightened and critical of its size.

We want a religious experience but are cool toward organized religion. We want philanthropy for the support of our causes, but we don't want any self-appointed groups to define the public good. We are aware how many of our aspirations and problems require joint action, but we are not comfortable with the existing vehicles of cooperation.

What has happened is that our attention to independence has overshadowed our attention to the interdependence so necessary to almost everything we want to accomplish. I suggest that we have now come to the absolutely essential next stage, which involves building a capacity for interdependence that will enhance, not stifle, our uniqueness as individuals and as a society; I believe that job is the role of the new leadership.

The urgent challenge facing all of us who are trying to find solutions to staggering public problems is to build or rebuild institutions capable of representing the interdependence of so many diverse people and causes.

If people and organizations concentrate on the things that divide us, or won't participate because the model or the vehicle isn't perfect, then we'll never get anywhere with the complex problems that beset us. It's so easy to criticize and so hard to lead, and the world and our institutions are imperfect, but we have to get behind the groups that are building and we have to begin to support much more than we tear down.

The job is not to level the institutions or to quiet the independent voices. The long, complex job facing the new leadership is to achieve an awareness of our interdependence and to build the vehicles for strengthening it while acknowledging the yearning and determination of people to be free. Harlan Cleveland, speaking at the tenth anniversary celebration of Common Cause, commented that "for the past twenty years, people have been ahead of their leaders." He cited as examples the environment, ecology, civil rights, women's issues, and the Vietnam War.[23]

The number of men and women passing these leadership tests is wonderfully encouraging. For proof of that, read David Broder's *Changing of the Guard*,[24] or visit almost any city or rural county and talk to the women and men who serve on the school boards, the health planning agencies, or other official and voluntary groups.

Today's leaders need to have these characteristics:

1. A passionate belief in participatory democracy, including the multiplication of participants and the dispersion of power.
2. A capacity both to enlarge and to survive the democratic cacophony in order to hear the individual shrieks—and songs.
3. An ability to educate the public, including the single-issue players, so that we are all better informed of the relationships between our special interests and the larger society in which those interests must be pursued.
4. An ability to make decisions, and to say no—even to you and to me.

In many ways, we are facing once again the eternal struggle of democratic governments to achieve a balance between freedom and order. The balancing effort is described by Henry Steele Commager in his preface to *Commager on Tocqueville*:

> Tocqueville's objective, so ardent and pervasive, so passionate that it was almost an obsession, was quite simply the future of liberty. He hence confronted that problem which has bemused political philosophers since Plato, the reconciliation of liberty and order. This is probably the greatest and most permanent problem in the whole history of government. . . . Would democratic majorities destroy liberty? Would centralization of power, which democracy made almost inevitable, prove incompatible with liberty? Would individualism—so ruthlessly being exercised on the vast North American continent—be compatible with either democracy or with liberty? And what of justice? There can be no liberty without justice and no justice without order. Can individualism tolerate order? Can democracy be trusted to safeguard justice?[25]

In *The Democratic Wish: Popular Participation and the Limits of American Government*, James A. Morone says that "the democratic wish" is for weak government and we therefore want multiple players, assuming that, because many of them are close to the local level, someone will be holding them accountable. In fact, Morone suggests that such a system gives citizens less influence. He suggests we should not be afraid of greater state power as long as it doesn't contradict our pluralistic approach but rather involves citizens more in defining and monitoring those systems.[26]

If, after years as a community organizer, I had to choose the one factor most likely to provide responsive, sensitive, effective service and systems, it would be consumer influence, especially consumer involvement in articulating needs, planning services, operating programs, and evaluating results. The more I work with communities, the more faith I develop in people's common sense and capacity to respond to responsibility fairly and practically.

Electing our officials is of course one of the best ways to keep government responsive to the people. But we need more attention to such basics as voter registration, voter turnout, regional governance, and the training of elected officials in their responsibilities, including maintaining the balance between prodding the system and supporting and interpreting it. Whatever the devices for encouraging rather than discouraging or neglecting citizen participation, the goal should be to give people maximum possible influence over the policies and programs designed to serve them.

John W. Gardner calls for new forms of governance. He says, "New patterns of governance are emerging. We use the word governance because it is so clear that government alone cannot bring our communities—or our nation—back to health." He elaborates:

> Today some of our cities are exhibiting an unprecedented purpose-fulness in tackling their own problems. It begins to look as though the future of the country will arise out of cities such as Minneapolis-St. Paul, Cleveland, Kansas City, Denver, Phoenix and Chattanooga. . . .
>
> Police commissioners are finding new ways to collaborate with neighborhood leaders, health care workers are forging new patterns of collaboration with the schools, corporations are working with job training programs. The patterns are infinitely varied. . . .
>
> There is urgent need for new patterns of collaboration among the governmental, business and nonprofit sectors, collaboration that includes neighborhood association, the professions, labor, minority groups, churches, schools, civic organizations and neighboring governmental jurisdictions.[27]

Nancy Kruh provides other good examples in "Across the United States, Citizens Are Discovering the Key to the Country's Social Problems Is Within Themselves," reported in the *Dallas Morning News*.

IN SEATTLE, a city fund of $1.5 million is distributed annually as seed money to neighborhoods who want to tackle their own problems. Citizens match the funds with volunteer labor, donated professional assistance and their own cash. Since 1987 the fund has supported hundreds of projects, including playgrounds, parks, community gardens and wildlife sanctuaries.

IN DALLAS, 60 churches . . . representing a racial, geographic and denominational cross-section of the area . . . have joined forces to work on such social issues as jobs, crime prevention and child care. Under the umbrella name, Dallas Area Interfaith, the year-old citizens' action group already has received $100,000 in city funds to set up after-school programs in six Dallas public schools, as well as commitments from private businesses to create more than 200 jobs.

IN DECATUR, GA, the homeless can sign up for free lunches for a month at a reservations-only cafe, complete with menu, fresh flowers and waiters. Besides the meals, the private, nonprofit cafe also provides free medical care, legal aid, resume service, counseling, AIDS awareness, 12-step programs and referrals to job-training. Since opening in 1986, the program has been run entirely by volunteers and donations.

But many Americans are finding their way back to their civic origins. To get there, they've taken a number of vehicles: the grassroots efforts, social experiments and trends that evolved in the 1970s and 1980s.

The story concludes:

Ultimately, say both scholars and research analysts, the movement may be less about citizenship and community than about what roles all three sectors . . . private, public and civic . . . should play in society. Indeed, many theorists believe all three are simultaneously attempting to redefine, realign and recalibrate themselves.

'People are searching for a new social compact,' said public issues researcher Richard Harwood. 'It revolves around our relationship to public institutions, and also, it involves the way we go about solving our problems. That's the interesting twist of the movement. It's not that people just want to get involved. They're trying to strike a new deal.'[28]

In a recent book, *Powered by Coalition*, I try to make the point that there is a pervasive and urgent need to figure out how to create such partnerships to deal with the growing complexity of needs in our communities and nation. People are finding increasingly that their causes are linked to others, and that solutions are not possible without allies. School dropouts and failures relate to inadequate nutrition, teen pregnancy, illiteracy, gangs, drugs, and so much more. International harmony is linked to control of nuclear power, reduction of hunger and famine, youth exchange, language training, and many other factors. Leaders of local governments or of single-issue causes, trying to improve schools, transportation systems or health care, realize they've got to link with others to have enough leverage to make a difference.[29]

Some of the most constructive innovations begin within government. For example:

- The annual winners of the Innovations in American Government competition co-sponsored by the Ford Foundation and the John F. Kennedy School of Government. A *Boston Globe* report on the 1997 winners indicated that government's new incarnation will be as a partner of citizens in problem solving.
- The Department of Housing and Urban Development's new job description for many of its staff is as "community builders," the equivalent of the federal government's long-standing success with the positions, title, and individuals identified as Agricultural Extension Agents who are universally recognized and received as friends and helpers.
- The International City/County Management Association (ICMA) operates the "Program for Community Problem Solving," which includes a substantial database of innovative programs that have worked and which have been written up for use by other communities. A unique part of this engagement is that it is tied to a television program and broader network called the "Civic Engagement Network," which in turn represents a fascinating and important example of the use of technology to advance replication of good ideas and programs developed elsewhere.

Another excellent resource for creative examples of community problem solving is the National Civic League's project and publication "Tales of Turnaround."[30]

A newer approach to building the capacity of communities to deal more effectively with their problems and aspirations is called "civic philanthropy." A number of funders are deciding that rather than devote all of their funds to specific programs or needs relating to health, the arts, or the environment, they will provide grants to help communities develop the "civic infrastructure" that will enable communities in turn to develop their own long-term solutions in just such areas as health, the arts, and the environment.

An important tool to help communities, including leaders of all three sectors—government, volunteer, and business—develop and evaluate their civic capacity is the "Civic Index" created by the National Civic League "to help communities evaluate and improve their civic infrastructures." The Civic Index components:

Citizen Participation

Community Leadership

Government Performance

Volunteerism and Philanthropy

Intergroup Relations

Civic Education

Community Information Sharing

Capacity for Cooperation and Consensus Building

Community Vision and Pride

Inter-Community Cooperation[31]

Finally I want to discuss the relationship of campaign finance reform to effective citizenship and government. Richard Goodwin recently summarized the crucial relationship this way:

> We talk about this as if it were an issue of "campaign finance reform," an obscure and somewhat technical subject. But that is not the issue at all. It is not about how politicians should be financed,

but how America should be governed, not about how we elect officials, but how they rule the nation.

The principal power in Washington is no longer the government or the people it represents. It is the money power. Under the deceptive cloak of campaign contributions, access, and influence, votes and amendments are bought and sold. Money establishes priorities of action, holds down federal revenues, revises federal legislation, shifts income from the middle class to the very rich. Money restrains the enforcement of laws written to protect the country from the abuses of wealth—laws that mandate environmental protection, antitrust laws, laws to protect the consumer against fraud, laws that safeguard the securities market, and many more. . . .

. . . The immediate issue is neither complicated nor difficult. But a little tinkering with "campaign finance laws," as is now proposed, will once again prove a travesty. We need to take the money out of politics before money takes the politics out of politics. The way to do this is through unavoidable and Draconian limits on giving and spending. . . .

. . . It will require today, as it has in the past, public protest and unrelenting exposure, a kind of national league against corruption, outside the parties and determined to drive from office all those who oppose reducing the power of wealth over our democracy.[32]

At the very least, in a representative democracy, elected officials must be responsible to their constituents for most functions of government. Greater engagement of citizens results in even more effective democracy. It comes down to effective citizenship → effective government → effective citizenship.

5

Volunteers, Voluntary Associations,
and Private Philanthropy:
The Independent Sector

There is a shared stake in the fundamental relationship between the freedom of citizens to organize
themselves and the freedom of citizens.
Organizing Committee Report,
INDEPENDENT SECTOR

Increasingly, we hear the lament that Americans don't really have
a civic spirit anymore. There is a pervasive view that we were
once far more willing than we are today to help one another and
to get involved in causes and public issues. It is almost a given that
we are now a less caring society and that we should worry about
what's happened to all that neighborliness, public spiritedness,
and charity.

Actually, from my knowledge and experience, the past was not
nearly as good as remembered and the present is far better than
perceived.

Fifty percent of all Americans are now active volunteers, and
they give an average of four hours a week to the causes of their
choice.

Three out of four of us are regular contributors of money to
charitable causes. We give more than one thousand dollars per

family each year. Almost 90 percent of the giving comes from individuals. Foundations and business corporations, as important as they are, represent only 10 percent of all that is contributed. People of all incomes are involved, and contributors at the lower end of the scale are more likely to be generous than the better off.[1]

We are the only country in the world where giving and volunteering are pervasive characteristics of so much of the population.

The base of participation is also spreading. There are more young people, more men, and more older people. Every economic group is involved. There are more people who have problems themselves.

The mutual help movement is the fastest growing side of the voluntary sector. For almost every problem, there is now a group of people who have weathered the storm and are reaching out to help others newly faced with loss of a child, depression, abuse, or heart surgery.

To the surprise of all who have matter-of-factly assumed that with so many women now in the work force it's harder to find female volunteers, the happy reality is that there are more women serving as volunteers. Indeed, several surveys provide the fascinating information that the woman who works for pay is more likely to volunteer than the woman who does not.

Volunteering obviously begins with the individual—the golden rule and lending a hand. Nathan Hale founded the Lend A Hand Society in 1885 and crafted its well-known credo.

> I am only one
> but at least I am one
> I cannot do everything
> But still I can do something
> And because I cannot do everything
> I will not refuse to do
> The something that I can do.[2]

One hundred million Americans are involved in an extraordinary array of acts of compassion and service. They inform, protest, assist, teach, heal, build, advocate, comfort, testify, support, solicit, donate, canvass, demonstrate, guide, feed, monitor, and in a hundred other ways serve people, communities, and causes.

Beyond all the indications of the good that results when so many people do so many good things, it is important to recognize what all these efforts mean to the kind of people we are. I submit that all this voluntary participation strengthens us as a nation, strengthens our communities, and strengthens and fulfills us as individual human beings. The Pulitzer Prize–winning historian Merle Curti says, "Emphasis on voluntary initiative has helped give America her national character."[3]

In writing *America's Voluntary Spirit*, I examined most of the great citizen crusades of our history. What came through again and again is that the participation, the caring, and the evidence that people can make a difference add wonderfully to the spirit of our society. For example, in "The Last Days of the Fight for Women's Suffrage" from *The Story of Alice Paul and the National Woman's Party*, Inez Haynes Irwin returns repeatedly to the spirit of those women. Not only were they able to decide on the task and accomplish it, but their success affected them as individual human beings. She says, for example, that "they developed a sense of comradeship for each other which was half love, half admiration and all reverence. In summing up a fellow worker, they speak first of her spirit and her spirit is always beautiful, or noble, or glorious."[4]

Incidentally (but hardly incidental), when one thinks of the giants of this voluntary sector, one is about as likely to think of women's as of men's names—at least in the past 150 years—names like Clara Barton, Jane Addams, Mary McLeod Bethune, Susan B. Anthony, Dorothea Dix, Alice Paul, Elizabeth Cady Stanton, Harriet Beecher Stowe, Dorothy Day, Mother Seton, Carrie Nation, Margaret Sanger, Lucretia Mott, and on and on. It's the only one of the three sectors that taps the full spectrum of the nation's talents.

The spirit of making a difference and comradeship emerges in most important voluntary activities. When individuals make the effort, not only do they help causes and people, but something special happens for them too; and in the composite, the individual, the community, and the nation take on a spirit of compassion, comradeship, and confidence.

Volunteers usually work together to increase their reach and results. There are more than a million charitable organizations officially registered with the Internal Revenue Service, ranging from small community groups to national crusades. And that number doesn't include most religious congregations, mutual assistance groups, or local chapters of large national organizations such as the American Cancer Society. Also not counted are the less formal groups concerned and involved with everything from prenatal care to cemeteries. Altogether the total is at least three million organizations and growing.

Voluntary organizations include major institutions such as universities, museums, and hospitals; large national crusades such as the American Heart Association and National Trust for Historic Preservation; and local associations dealing with almost every possible cause and concern. INDEPENDENT SECTOR's classification of tax exempt organizations covers twenty-five divisions or fields of interest such as health, recreation, international, religion, and education; and thousands of causes such as learning difficulties, animals, pollution, dance, refugees, and bail assistance.[5] In *People Power* I describe three general purposes of philanthropic and voluntary organizations; service (such as youth hostels), advocacy (such as Americans for Indian Opportunity), and empowerment (such as the National Organization for Women).[6]

In preparing this book, I was fascinated to find how many authors emphasize the role of voluntary institutions as training grounds for democratic involvement. Sara Evans and Harry Boyte write: "Free spaces can thus be evaluated in terms of their effectiveness as schools for democracy"[7]; Helen Ingram and Stephen Rathgeb Smith say, "Citizenship develops through association, and although associations can introduce the evils of faction, they can also be schools for democracy."[8]

In chapter 2, I introduced the point that communities and voluntary organizations provide individuals with interconnections to extend almost every important element of their private lives, including religious expression and mutually beneficial projects. A great many of these relationships are informal, but many require some structure, which leads to the creation of associations.

Whether one's interest is wildflowers or civil rights, arthritis or clean air, oriental art or literacy, the dying or the unborn, organizations are already at work; and if they don't suit our passion, it's a wonderful fact of America that we can go out and start our own.

Robert Wuthnow, who tracks the development of smaller

voluntary groups, says that "small groups connect us to larger communities."[9] He points out that forty percent of all Americans belong to such groups, which now number in the millions.

> The large number of people who are involved in small groups, the depth of their involvement, the extent of their caring for each other, and even the degree to which they reach out to others in the wider community all suggest that the social fabric has not unraveled nearly to the extent that many critics have suggested. . . . The attachments that develop among the members of small groups demonstrate clearly that we are not a society of rugged individualists who wish to go it entirely alone but, rather, that we are a communal people who, even amidst the dislocating tendencies of our society, are capable of banding together in bonds of mutual support.[10]

Wuthnow and others indicate that the number, variety, and importance of small groups provides the basic network of social activity and for learning the organizational skills to tackle larger tasks. Though the groups start out, and may remain, focused on mutual interests such as hobbies, sports, or the Bible, their "social talk" often deals with broader subjects leading to awareness and action.

Berry, Portney, and Thomson found that "There is a strong and positive relationship between the level of participation and sense of community."[11]

Before discussing the activities and results of larger associations and movements, it seems important to reflect briefly on how much the right and habit of association mean to the liberties of Americans and even to the survival of our democracy. James Luther Adams, one of the most articulate writers on collective action, says, "it has been voluntary associations which have impressed upon the community and the state the demands for democratic rights."[12]

In *Beyond Preference: Liberal Theories of Independent Associations*, Franklin I. Gamwell says that voluntary associations should be known as the "first sector" because they "are essential to the full realization of human capacities" and that "public-regarding associations are, to appropriate the words of Tocqueville, not only as necessary to the American people as all others, but more so."[13]

John Gardner says that "almost every major social breakthrough in America has originated in this voluntary sector." He continues:

If volunteers and voluntary organizations were to disappear from our national life, we would be less distinctly American. The sector enhances our creativity, enlivens our communities, nurtures individual responsibility, stirs life at the grassroots, and reminds us that we were born free. Its vitality is rooted in good soil—civic pride, compassion, a philanthropic tradition, a strong problem-solving impulse, a sense of individual responsibility, and an irrepressible commitment to the great shared task of improving our life together.[14]

Another benefit of voluntary association is somewhat intangible but vital. It is probably illustrated best by an encounter within the organizing committee of the world alliance CIVICUS. We were trying to determine specific activities the new organization would emphasize, such as influence with the United Nations, international conferences, newsletters, and research, when one of our members burst out that we were totally missing the mark. This was Farida Allaghi, an exile from Libya working out of Saudi Arabia to try to establish women's rights in the Middle East. Farida had faithfully attended all our meetings but was frequently disparaging of our attention to organizational detail. Now she demanded that we not bother her or ourselves with silly talk of conferences or newsletters because, as she reproached us, "the only issue is courage."

From the chair, I wanted terribly to respond to the obvious depth of her feelings, but I was dumbfounded, as I could tell the others were, about what she was trying to convey. Within that awkward moment, Farida, trembling with frustration and anger, grabbed her papers and started to leave. Several rose to stop her, and I tried to speak for all of us in an earnest plea for her to help us understand what it was that upset her so.

Still standing and somewhere between disconsolate and furious, Farida explained that she came to these gatherings only because she found in the group others who were struggling against almost impossible odds to address human rights and trying to survive oppressive governments, and that with every indication of progress she picked up from the group, she was able to return to her awful circumstances with a little more courage. "Please," she pleaded, "don't ever let us get so preoccupied with the details that we forget what this is all about which is giving a little more hope and courage to people who spend a lot of their time wondering if they can possibly go on."

Farida's lesson may seem distant for many of us who are not dealing with unbearable circumstances, but even in this country, organizers and organizations need encouragement especially to confront new or renewed obstacles and threats to their causes.

When INDEPENDENT SECTOR was formed, we emphasized the need for independence of citizen organizations.

> There are many roles and values that voluntary organizations represent, including providing services and acting as vehicles through which the government fulfills some of its public responsibilities, but the largest contribution, by far, is the independence these organizations represent for innovation, excellence, criticism and, where necessary, reform.[15]

It is usually the combination of independence and numbers of people that give this sector its power. In *Rules for Radicals*, Saul Alinsky says "Change comes from power, and power comes from organization. In order to act, people must get together."[16]

It is this joining together of compassion, spirit, and power that often makes the difference for the most serious issues facing all of us. Such enormous and complicated problems as cancer and poverty require thousands of volunteers focusing on service, prevention, public awareness, and public policy.

Usually when people cite examples of the sector's power and impact, they refer to the distant past, to such issues as slavery, women's suffrage, and child labor laws. As important as those examples are, their constant repetition tends to support the notion that significant things are less likely to occur today. It is my distinct experience that in just the past twenty-five years, there has been an absolute explosion of citizen impact on a vast range of human consideration. We organize to serve every conceivable aspect of the human condition and are willing to stand up and be counted on almost any public issue. We mobilize to fight zoning changes, approve bond issues, improve garbage collection, expose overpricing, enforce equal rights, and protest wars. Our interest and impact extend from neighborhoods to the ozone layer and beyond.

In my 1999 book *Voices from the Heart: In Celebration of America's Volunteers*,[17] I provided indications of very recent and very profound involvement and impact. Here is a sampling of such breakthroughs:

In just the past twenty years, volunteers have broken through centuries of indifference to the needs of the dying, and as a result of their noble crusade, almost every community today has hospice services providing relief to the terminally ill and their families.

In very recent times, volunteers' passion, courage, and tenacity have forced the nation and every region in it to realize that we must preserve for future generations our precious resources of water, air, and land. That ethic and practice now affect every form of local and national asset, including wetlands, forests, farmland, historic buildings, and whole downtowns.

Volunteers stood up and were counted for common decency and adequate services for retarded children, and those break-throughs showed the way to many others who then dared to do the same for cerebral palsy, autism, learning disabilities, and hundreds of other problems we hadn't even heard of twenty years ago.

With the establishment and growth of Alcoholics Anonymous, volunteers pioneered a model of mutual assistance that today extends to almost every serious personal problem. In almost every community there's a group of people who have weathered the storm and are reaching out to others newly faced with such crises as a child's death, mastectomy, depression, stroke, or physical abuse.

Volunteers sang "we are not afraid," though of course they were—but with each new volunteer recruited to the civil rights crusade, their courage, confidence, and power grew, and then when their vast army sang and believed "we shall overcome," they did. The civil rights movement then spread to every disenfranchised and underrepresented group, including women, the physically disabled, Native Americans, Hispanics, gays, and so many more.

A few volunteers, at first mostly parents and students, believed they could do something about drunk driving, but despite its escalating ravages, most of us didn't think they would succeed. Thank God they did. With that evidence of the power of ordinary people, more individuals realized that maybe—just maybe—they could also change public policies and behavior about smoking, and look what they've done.

Dealing with community problems was one thing, but some issues defied organization or were off limits for reasons of national security. However, some people believed that matters such as control of nuclear power were linked to survival, and they stepped in, at their peril, to reduce our peril.

Volunteers even began to take peace into their territory with people-to-people understanding as a fundamental step to reduce international tensions and build tolerance and friendship.

And all the time a healthy number of people served all of us by promoting the importance and availability of arts and cultural opportunities as central aspects of a civilized society. One of the great waves of voluntary activity and impact has involved community theater, dance, and music to provide opportunities for creativity and enjoyment of it.

The list goes on almost endlessly with preschool education, day care, social services, cancer control, consumerism, population control, conflict resolution, ethnic museums, early infant care, independent living for the elderly, teen pregnancy, AIDS, substance abuse, job training, and so very much more.

For those who believe that, because we have not yet been able to fix all of these problems, there must be a flagging of capacity for public problem solving, I point out that most of the problems we now face are the most complex, intransigent issues with which people have ever struggled. To conquer them will test all of our commitment, tenacity, ingenuity, and organizational skills.

The whole chapter and indeed the whole book could be profitably devoted to the social role of religions and their congregations. They are everywhere, including at the center of our caring society. Fifty percent of charitable contributions goes to congregations, and that doesn't count religiously affiliated schools, hospitals, and social services. Of the 50 percent, approximately half flows through the congregation to people in need. Eighteen percent of all volunteering is congregation-related and much more is brought about by the teaching and encouragement of religions and their leaders.

As a community organizer, I am keenly aware of the significance of congregations as a source of valuable volunteering for all sorts of community activities. They were always my first stop when I went into a community to start a new activity. Because I've had such a favorable experience and have such a positive view of the community services of churches, synagogues, mosques and their counterparts, I am always surprised and disappointed when I hear people dismiss religions as a core part of our independent sector, relegating them to the separate and singular category of personal salvation. At an early stage of the organization of INDE-PENDENT SECTOR there was a serious move to omit religions be-cause, as the argument went, they were not really voluntary organ-izations. Fortunately, those of us who had extensive field experience knew how terribly inadequate our representation would have been without them.

Congregations are the first line of service to their neighbor-hoods far beyond their own memberships, and the poorer the neighborhood, the more likely and larger the service. If one looks at what the conscience, the meeting ground, and the organized neighborliness represented by religious congregations mean to the kind of society America is, religion takes on a different and larger significance. And we don't have to go back in history for ex-amples. Who has been more in the forefront of the public business of the homeless, spousal abuse, hunger and the resettlement of refugees?

In their writings on "Mediating Structures," Berger and Neu-haus count churches, broadly defined, as one of the most powerful of mediating institutions.[18] In *Voice and Equality*, Verba, Schloz-man, and Brady write:

> those with high levels of educational attainment are likely to be slotted into the kinds of prestigious and lucrative jobs and organ-izational affiliations that provide further political resources. Only religious institutions provide a counterbalance to this cumulative resource process. They play an unusual role in the American par-ticipatory system by providing opportunities for the development of civic skills to those who would otherwise be resource-poor.[19]

Finally, I turn to private philanthropy including the support provided by foundations and businesses. Though most charitable giving comes from individuals (almost 90 percent), the rest, given by organized philanthropy, is also tremendously important, espe-cially as seed capital. Paul Ylvisaker, an educator, community acti-vist, and foundation official described such philanthropy as "America's passing gear."

In *Philanthropy in Action*, my opening chapter is called "Philanthropy: America's Extra Dimension"; in part, I said: "Philanthropy plays many different roles in our society, but its central value is the extra dimension it provides for seeing and doing things differently."[20] For the book I tried to identify several of the different though admittedly overlapping roles that philanthropy in general plays and ended up with nine. At times in this exercise there were four or five and other times seventeen or eighteen, so clearly there is nothing sacred in the delineation and enumeration of the roles.

- To Discover New Frontiers of Knowledge
- To Support and Encourage Excellence
- To Enable People to Exercise Their Potential
- To Relieve Human Misery
- To Preserve and Enhance Democratic Government and Institutions
- To Make Communities a Better Place to Live
- To Nourish the Spirit
- To Create Tolerance, Understanding, and Peace among People
- To Remember the Dead

I might have settled for just two roles—To Relieve Human Misery and To Maximize Human Potential—but the extended list allowed a closer examination of the various ways that charitable giving makes a difference. If I had been really pressed to reduce it to just one role, it would have been "To Serve as America's Extra Dimension."

It might help to illuminate and enliven personal philanthropy, foundations, and corporate giving to provide a few examples from *Philanthropy in Action*.

When I was growing up in Worcester, Massachusetts, we had a neighbor who was considered odd because he kept trying to put rockets in the air. Almost nobody thought he could do it; the few who did worried that he could cause perpetual rain or bring the sky falling in or shoot an angel.

Robert H. Goddard was known derisively as "the moon man." In 1920 he made the laughable prediction that a rocket could go to the moon. For years the only money he had for research came from his own pocket. His first grant came in 1917, a five-thousand-dollar gift from the Hodgkins Fund of the Smithsonian

Institution for "constructing and launching a high altitude rocket." Nine years later his modest attempt to fulfill the terms of that grant rose forty-one feet and flew for 2.5 seconds—just far enough to encourage Goddard and just a short enough distance to discourage funders.

In 1929 a larger model blasted off, literally and figuratively. The explosion did send his missile one hundred feet up but started a fire several thousand feet wide. Most of the press attention focused on the fire, but a few stories marveled at the accomplishment; one of these articles was read by Mrs. Harry Guggenheim.

The history of Goddard's rocketry and the Guggenheims' support are nicely captured in Milton Lomask's *Seed Money: The Guggenheim Story.* Lomask reports that the culmination of Goddard's work was a rocket that became "the parent of all the 9000 mile Adases and Redstones that will ever fly, all the Sputniks that will ever circle planet earth, all the Project Mercury, Saturn and Jupiter capsules that will ever soar to Venus, Moon and Mars."[21]

There don't seem to be figures on how much Goddard received from various sources for his lifetime of research, but it probably was a good deal less than half a million dollars. Matched against what his work has led to, it is appropriate that the Guggenheim story is told under the heading, "Seed Money."

Another good example relates to the founding of Stanford University. When word reached the East Coast in 1885 that Leland Stanford was considering founding a college in the West to rank with Harvard and Columbia, a New York newspaper responded, "California needs a great university about like Switzerland needs a navy."

Leland and Jane Stanford had only one child, Leland Stanford, Jr. He was born late in their lives, but soon became the center of their activity. He traveled with them on almost all their extensive trips. On a trip to Italy he contracted typhoid fever and died shortly before his sixteenth birthday. According to the history of Stanford: "Governor Stanford, who had remained at Leland's bedside continuously, fell into a troubled sleep the morning the boy died. When he awakened he turned to his wife and said, 'The children of California shall be our children.' "[22]

The rest of the story is well known, except perhaps one often overlooked point—that from the start, Stanford University was to admit women, which brought more response from the East: "Can you imagine such audacity as that?"

In his 1951 Founders' Day address "The Power of Freedom" at Johns Hopkins University, Henry Allen Moe, early leader of the John Simon Guggenheim Memorial Foundation, spoke of the role of philanthropy in the support of talent.

here and there stands out one who exemplifies, in Bertrand Russell's words, "all the noon-day brightness of human genius . . ."

To develop and bring to their highest possible exercise the capacities of individual persons to make that voyage is, quite obviously, the world's most needed result. Only thus shall we add that knowledge and understanding which is our best hope for survival and progress. All universities and all foundations should know they miss all their best opportunities if they fail to recognize that this should be their one goal, and that it is the only goal within their reach.[23]

I mentioned earlier that philanthropy might be divided into two roles: maximizing human potential and relieving human misery. Some of the best projects bridge the two, such as efforts at literacy.

In a 1953 history of the Anna T. Jeanes Fund, written by its president, Arthur D. Wright, there is this report of a 1907 meeting of Jeanes with Hollis B. Frisell, president of Hampton Institute, Booker T. Washington, head of Tuskegee Institute, and George Peabody, officer of the General Education Board:

"Dost thee remember that thee didst call upon me and that I gave thee a check?"

"Yes, well do I remember, Miss Jeanes, your fine generosity," said Mr. Frisell.

"And dost thee remember that I gave thee a like sum, Dr. Washington?"Booker T. Washington assented in like manner.

"And dost thee remember that thee didst write me about making a gift to the General Education Board?"

"Yes, indeed, I do," said Mr. Peabody, "and I am grateful for the privilege of sharing in this rich opportunity for service."

"Thee does not need to thank me. It is I who needs to thank thee,"—and with a flash of spirit she added— "and I didn't do it to save my soul from Hell either!"

With that introduction to their discussion, Anna T. Jeanes, elderly, plain living, plain talking, Philadelphia Quaker "turned over a million dollars in securities establishing The Negro Rural School Fund to help the poorest and most isolated black children in the South to read and write." Jeanes was, in her own words, "guided by a God of love and peace." She believed that what the best of religion teaches is that giving is not a sacrifice but the happy extension of a generous deity. Thus she also meant "and I didn't do it to save my soul from Hell, either!"[24]

If it's true that God loves a cheerful giver, he must also have a particularly warm spot for Dr. D. K. Pearsons, who gave everything away, and did it in good spirit. For example, when Pearsons sent the enormous sum of fifty thousand dollars to Montpelier Seminary in Vermont in 1912. He appended this note:

> Fifty-thousand dollars farewell!
> You have been in my keeping for many years,
> and you have been a faithful servant . . . go into the
> keeping of young men and God's blessing go with you!
> Do your duty, and give the poor boys and girls of
> Vermont a fair chance.[25]

William G. Rogers in *Ladies Bountiful* comments on assistance given to James Joyce by Lady Gregory for whom Joyce coined this limerick:

> There was a kind lady called Gregory
> Said, "Come to me, poets in beggary,"
> But found her imprudence
> When thousands of students
> Cried, "all, we are in that category."[26]

Perhaps the most universally applauded grants to America's communities were Andrew Carnegie's gifts of 1,680 libraries. Despite the obvious merit of those facilities and our awareness, a hundred years later, of their contribution to learning, the grants were often viewed with suspicion and hostility. Many community leaders said that they saw through his condition that if he paid for the building, they would have to buy the books and maintain the service. In place after place, the gifts were attacked on the grounds that ordinary people didn't need to read, would steal all the books anyway, or should be satisfied with their school books. In his book *Philanthropy's Role in Civilization*, Arnaud C. Marts reports that in one community, these signs appeared:

> Ratepayers!
> Resist this free library dodge and
> save yourself from the burden of 6,000
> of additional taxation![27]

Marts also reports that for many years even the progressive state of Massachusetts prohibited any municipality from taxing people for the support of a library. He adds that "The son of a president of Harvard published a book in 1875 in which he endeavored to dissuade his fellow citizens against appropriations for libraries."[28]

The history of philanthropy is full of grants that we can't possibly imagine were controversial, but which in their time seemed radical and ill advised. Massachusetts was on the better side of the controversy involving kindergartens, but most other states saw that movement as sinister. Elizabeth Peabody of Boston, a sister of Horace Mann, donated her own funds and raised money from her friends to establish the first English-speaking kindergarten.

It is hard to fathom that kindergartens could have been threatening to anyone, but Peabody started a very long and bitter dispute. Her attackers said that children that age were too young to learn and belonged in the home anyway, that her idea undermined the family, transferred to the state a private responsibility and would raise taxes that were already too high or were needed for "real" public services. The cries of bloated government and encouraging family dependence on government caused many states to enact laws prohibiting the use of public school funds or other taxes to be used on children of kindergarten age. It took about fifty years for the program to gain acceptance.

A hundred years after Peabody's first kindergarten, Carnegie's foundation, the Carnegie Corporation of New York, tried to take the idea a step further by funding "Head Start," a program for disadvantaged children of prekindergarten age, and thirty years later the fur is still flying. Will day care be next?

One of the newer lessons about philanthropy involves the breadth of ways in which corporate philanthropy is becoming involved. At a Council on Foundations meeting, Alex Plinio, then director of contributions for Prudential, gave a paper with a title like, "Fourteen Ways That Companies Provide Non-cash Assistance to Voluntary Organizations." I urged him to expand it into a more formal article and told him that INDEPENDENT SECTOR would be pleased to publish it.

About a year later, I asked Alex how it was coming and he kept finding new examples that should be included. By then, he was up to "Twenty-Nine Ways . . ." He also had been promoted to vice-president for public service and president of the Prudential Foundation, so he had even less time to work on the paper. Finding the idea more interesting than ever and sharing his frustration with his time constraints, I said we would provide him with some research and editorial assistance. Another year went by, and I explained to him that we really should be getting something published. This time Alex said that between his own efforts and those of Joanne Scanlan, the part-time assistant, he was coming across all kinds of new information that really should be included. By then, he was up to "Forty-One Ways . . ."

Six months later, out of eagerness to have this important resource document published and seeing my offer of modest help reach a not-so-modest level, I said we absolutely had to go with what he had. The result was Plinio and Scanlon's excellent *Resource Raising: The Role of Non-Cash Assistance in Corporate Philanthropy*, which contains forty-nine types of assistance and more than one hundred examples.[29] At that, Plinio still says, "You know, Brian, I wish we hadn't rushed into print. It's still very incomplete!"

Their paper graphically illustrates how different corporate philanthropy is from the work of private foundations. *Resource Raising* contains information about an extraordinary variety of in-kind gifts or subsidies that corporations are currently providing to nonprofit organizations. These include loaned executives, gifts of land, computer tie-ins, piggy-back advertising, dispute resolution and negotiation services, energy conservation audits, product and marketing consultation, survey development and analysis, gifts of trees, horses, and seeds, no-interest or low-interest loans, meeting and conference facilities, and staff and volunteer training.

As important as in-kind gifts are, they are still only a supplement to the dollar support that corporations represent. I was reminded of this during one of the public meetings of the Minnesota Council on Foundations when one of the corporate speakers went on and on about how much a growing number of companies were doing to provide non-cash support. The already lively discussion ended with applause and whistles when one of the voluntary agency representatives rose to observe, "With all due respect for your non-cash help, I hope you won't get so carried away with it that you forget the cash!"

One of the best descriptions I've heard of how a business corporation should target its charitable giving grew out of a 1978 study by the Weyerhaeuser paper products company. Prompted by concerns that the corporation had been donating money to projects too far removed from the company's identifiable interests and strengths, Weyerhaeuser reviewed its public service program, taking the opportunity to study the rationale and priorities of its future program.

After hearing and considering all the advice about being truly public-serving or truly self-serving, the company concluded, as William Ruckelshaus, then Weyerhaeuser vice-president, described it, "that they should be at the intersection of corporate self-interest and societal need." Since then, the company has moved "toward topics of unique concern to the Company, but important to the larger society as well."[30] Following those guidelines, the company decided to give considerable attention and money to preservation of forests, a topic it knows a great deal about and has a stake in.

Corporations initially started to support voluntary efforts through this same enlightened self-interest. In *Corporation Giving*, F. Emerson Andrews recalls a case in which there was a literal crossroads. The railroad companies found a need to help develop local YMCAs to provide for their employees "supervised, economical accommodations." Both sides saw a distinct advantage to the relationship. Andrews reports that by the 1890s, YMCAs were established at eighty-two divisional and terminal crossroads.[31]

One of the best answers to whether it is the business of business to give anything away and even whether such behavior works against the interests of stockholders was provided by James Burke, chairman of Johnson and Johnson, when he and his company received the Advertising Council's 1983 Public Service Award. As described in INDEPENDENT SECTOR's *Corporate Philanthropy*, Burke said "Those companies that organize their business around the broad concept of public service, over the long run provide superior performance for their stockholders." Burke's conclusions were drawn from a survey of companies that had received the Ad Council award. He noted:

> These companies showed an annual 11 percent growth in profits compounded over 30 years! That happens to be better than three times the growth of the Gross National Product . . . which grew at 3.1 percent annually during the same period.
>
> If anyone had invested $30,000 in a composite of the Dow Jones 30 years ago, it would be worth $134,000 today. If you had invested the same $30,000 . . . $2,000 in each of these companies instead . . . your $30,000 would be worth over $1 million . . . $1,021,861 to be exact!

Burke summarized,

> I have long harbored the belief that the most successful corporations in this country—the ones that have delivered outstanding results over a long period of time—were driven by a simple moral imperative—serving the public in the broadest possible sense—better than their competition. . . . We as businessmen and women have extraordinary leverage on our most important asset . . . the goodwill of the public . . . if we make sure our enterprises are managed in terms of their obligations to society . . . that is also the best way to defend this democratic, capitalistic system that means so much to all of us.[32]

Another lesson that comes through my own review of private philanthropy is the tenaciousness, patience, and farsightedness it takes to stay with a problem until it is solved. The Rockefeller Foundation funded research that identified hookworm as the underlying cause of so many of the health problems of rural poor; they then established a National Sanitary Commission to solve the problem, and then they established many similar state commissions to do the necessary local field work.

The Rockefeller Foundation has been applying that same stick-to-it-iveness to the endless, almost thankless task of encouraging greater attention to the humanities. Their point, so long-range that even a foundation with its record has a hard time holding the course, is that in the end, there will be more discovery, learning, and maybe even peace if we strive now for stronger scholarship in such fields as history, philosophy, languages, and theology.

Sometimes the hardest ones look easier than they are and turn out to require several lifetimes of investment. Early in this century, Andrew Carnegie established The Endowment for International Peace and provided his trustees with advice on what to do with his money when they had finished the job. The endowment was to have been the capstone of Carnegie's philanthropic endeavors, but even his optimism and resources were no match for serious international problems. Philip E. Mosely, writing on "International Affairs" in Warren Weaver's *U.S. Philanthropic Foundations*, captures nicely the Carnegie spirit:

> In establishing the Carnegie Endowment for International Peace in 1910, Andrew Carnegie sincerely believed that the permanent elimination of wars and prospect of wars might well be achieved in the lifetime of men then living. He directed the Trustees, when that happy state had been achieved, to apply the Endowment's resources to solve other major problems of mankind.[33]

What followed, of course, was not peace but two slaughtering world wars, the development of nuclear weapons, Korea, Vietnam, the Middle East, and a whole world that could explode at any moment. Andrew Carnegie, where are you?

It is encouraging that ninety years later Carnegie's foundation, the Carnegie Corporation of New York, is picking up the challenge with an endeavor to try to end war.

Most of the great social movements of our society involved courageous philanthropists and volunteers involved with abolition of slavery, women's suffrage, creation of public libraries, care and opportunities for the disabled and on and on. Many who led those efforts were viewed as unpopular, troublesome, rabble-rousing and maybe even dangerous. One of the hallmarks of philanthropy is its support for unpopular people and ideas and protection of their freedom.

It is unreasonable and even inappropriate to expect that all philanthropic organizations will be on the "cutting edge." Though much of the good that philanthropy does is accomplished on the edge, many funders find themselves simply encouraging organizations toward excellence, intervening where human misery is greatest, or nourishing the human spirit.

Philanthropy plays many different roles in our society, but its central value is the extra dimension it provides for seeing and doing things differently. Philanthropy doesn't take the place of government or other basic institutions, but its impact is clear in just about every field of endeavor, including fields as different as architecture, health, human rights, historic preservation, ballet, neighborhood empowerment, agriculture, rocketry, physics, the homeless, astronomy—and peace.

Oliver Wendell Holmes observed, "Philanthropists are commonly grave, occasionally grim and not very rarely morose."[34] From my long review of their accomplishments, I think philanthropists have reason to be happier with what they do.

As the next chapter indicates, not everything that happens in the independent sector or in the broader civil society is necessarily good, however. Their champions need to acknowledge that the very pluralism that provides the freedom for so many good things to happen also opens room for activities that are foolish, counterproductive, or downright threatening to the rights of others. The constant task is to maintain the freedoms while improving our ability to evaluate performance and deal forcefully with the transgressors.

6

Limitations of Civil Society, Threats to It, and the General State of It

> Civil society is something much easier for the state to
> destroy than to construct.
>
> FRANCIS FUKUYAMA

As founding president of INDEPENDENT SECTOR, and having made civil society my life's work, it's obvious I am a believer. What may not be so obvious is that these years and experiences have also taught me a great deal about civil society's limitations.

There's a real problem, for example, in getting a firm grasp on it. It's even hard to quantify in terms of income, expenditures, and tangible products. As a result, we are up in the air on such essential matters as how to measure civil society's effectiveness and whether we could depend on it even more to address public tasks. It's also hard to know civil society's boundaries. For example, how much of government or business is in, out, or somewhat related to it? That sometimes leads to severe exaggerations of its size and capacity.

Research will eventually tell us far more about size and scope, but I'll go out on a limb and predict that civil society will turn out to appear decidedly small, at least in the tangible measurements of dollars and employees, compared with its social contributions. We already know a good deal, for instance, about the size of the country's independent sector, which is likely to be a large part of any measurement of civil society, and we know that the independent sector is very small compared with commerce and government. The total income of voluntary institutions and associations is only 6 percent of National Income, compared with 15 percent for government and 79 percent for commerce. The comparison becomes even starker when one measures the total expenditures of nonprofit organizations against the expenditures of government. According to INDEPENDENT SECTOR's *Nonprofit Almanac*, nonprofit groups spent approximately $357 billion in 1990, contrasted with the combined expenditures of the three levels of government of about $3.5 trillion.[1] Thus, nonprofit expenditures are only about 10 percent the size of government expenditures and of this, approximately one-third comes from government in the form of contracts and fees for service.

The service role of nonprofit organizations is substantially funded by government, for example maternal and child health, job training, and care of the elderly, which makes many of these voluntary groups more governmental than independent. A greater transfer of government's responsibilities and funds will diminish further the independence that is the sector's most important attribute.

In *People Power*, I wrote that the impacts of voluntarism can generally be categorized as service, advocacy, and empowerment, and although each is important, the relative worth to society is in inverse proportion to the dollars available. An increased emphasis on the service role, such as trying to take on more of government's human services, will mean that the service part of the sector, in terms of money and employees, will dwarf and obscure the remainder, and this will reinforce the impression that service is what the sector is and does. As important as those direct services are, they are, to my mind and experience, decidedly secondary to the functions of advocacy and empowerment, where the dollars and staff are comparatively tiny, but where the contributions to civil society and democracy are immense.[2]

Several years ago I attended a Ditchley Foundation Conference in England that had an ambitious title, such as The Future of Philanthropy in the Western World, and it became clear that for other countries the total amounts of money represented by voluntary organizations are absolutely minuscule compared to their governments. For example, in Britain, the total voluntary sector is about 2 percent the size of government compared with our 10 percent, and foundation and corporate grants are an almost invisible fraction of 1 percent. Even at that, representatives from those other countries argued that however small the percentage and even the money amounts might be, they provide absolutely vital elements of flexibility, innovation, creativity, and capacity for criticism and reform and therefore must be preserved.

One of the issues discussed at that meeting was whether philanthropic monies should be used to supplement government expenditures, particularly at a time of government cutbacks. At that time, both Prime Minister Thatcher and President Reagan were urging private philanthropy to make up for some government retrenchment. Many United States mayors were also urging foundations and corporations to help government keep schools, libraries, and parks open and to maintain other public services. During and after those discussions, it became clear that although philanthropy has a responsibility to deal with emergency matters, particularly those involving human suffering, in the long run the small amounts that philanthropy contributes must be reserved for *extra* purposes. If not, philanthropic expenditures will not represent anything unique and therefore might not be worth preserving.

Another reality and limitation is that the broader civil society is not really accountable to anybody. Even the courts, though they have some influence, cannot ensure that civil society will function as a democratic society needs it to. Who, if anyone, should be accountable? If no one, who defends civil society from everyone? Civil society, as a related issue, does not really have a constituency, or at least one that accepts the burden of stewardship and mission. Everyone is a participant, but no one is trustee.

Another set of limitations evolves from this lack of permanent leadership and responsibility. For example, much of the best that happens in civil society relates to major citizen crusades, but democratic movements are hard to sustain. In *Free Spaces*, Evans and Boyte comment that "democratic movements have had varying degrees of success in sustaining themselves, in spreading their values, symbols, and ideas to larger audiences, in changing the world."[3] They also remind us that citizen movements are not always healthy and they serve up such vivid examples as the Ku Klux Klan, the White Citizens Council, and those who would save us from "dangerous books."[4]

In *Voice and Equality*, Verba, Schlozman, and Brady make clear that inequality of participation is a decided limitation of civic voluntarism.

However, so long as inequalities in education and income persist—
and income inequality in America has become more pronounced of
late—so long as jobs continue to distribute opportunities to practice civic skills in a stratified manner, then individuals will continue
to command stockpiles of participatory factors of very different
sizes and, thus, to participate at very different rates. . . . Because political participation is so deeply rooted in the essential structures of
American society, we can expect that the voices heard through the
medium of citizen participation will be often loud, sometimes clear,
but rarely equal.[5]

In *The Rebirth of Urban Democracy*, Berry, Portney, and Thomson
suggest that undue dependence on voluntary alliances detracts
from proper attention to making government effective. "Neighborhood associations are creative mechanisms for tying people
into their communities. . . . Nevertheless, America needs more
people involved in politics and government."[6]

As much as I believe in voluntary initiative, we lose our perspective when we exaggerate its importance, particularly when we
put it ahead of the roles of democratic government and our responsibility to it. Similarly, we make a mistake if we exaggerate
what voluntary action can do, particularly if it allows us to exaggerate what government need not do.

Many of the *threats* to our civil society relate to the misunderstanding of what it is and its relevance to the functions and preservation of democracy. Hodgkinson defines this part of the problem
as our "crisis of information," which she believes is so serious that
it is more accurately labeled "the state of our ignorance."[7]

The history of other democracies teaches us that the greatest
threat often comes from within—from the inattention and neglect of its citizens. Recall Edmund Burke's, "The only thing necessary for the triumph of evil is for good men [and women] to do
nothing."[8]

At times it is government that is guilty of the neglect, intended or otherwise. Several years ago I was approached by a
committee made up of representatives of Jewish organizations in
the United States and Israel to participate in a study of why more
aspects of civil society including a strong independent sector had

not developed in Israel. I agreed to participate in part because I was fascinated that what we generally describe as the Judeo-Christian influence on our civil society seemed to be missing in the Jewish homeland.

The committee was inclined to believe that the absence of tax incentives for charitable giving might be the major cause and that the problem might be solved by legislation. I explained that studies of the United States system made clear that people do not contribute because of the charitable deduction. They contribute instead to help people, communities, and causes; but the availability of some deduction increases the *size* of such gifts. The group listened to my thoughts but asked me to keep an open mind.

I wasn't far into my review when I realized that in its first fifty years Israel and its people were necessarily preoccupied with pressing needs such as building governmental systems of defense, roads, education, and housing. These had to be their focus. However, fifty years later they were surprised to realize that Israel had a limited independent sector. They did have a great many quasi-governmental institutions, but these were really the government's way of doing its public business and were too dependent on government to be considered independent. Now Israel is far more aggressive in attending to the development of a truly *independent* voluntary structure, including the establishment of an organization along the lines of our INDEPENDENT SECTOR. That experience has always stood out as a warning that even people committed to voluntary action can neglect this central aspect of civil society.

In the United States, our civil society is constantly at risk because so many policymakers and administrators within government do not understand or, worse, are unsympathetic and even hostile to such notions as pluralism and advocacy. In a paper presented to the National Academy of Public Administration, "The Relationship Between Voluntary Organizations and Government: Constructive Partnerships/Creative Tensions," I tried to get across that there is about as much confusion and competition as most of us can handle in just trying to build and blend our service delivery mechanisms, without getting into the advocacy role of nonprofit organizations, but that if we really want to understand and shape the broader context of how government services are decided and provided, we have to develop an even higher tolerance for the pain sugar-coated as "creative tension."[9]

In another paper, "What Voluntary Activity Can and Cannot Do for America,"[10] I tried to explain how these misunderstandings of pluralism and voluntary initiative end up damaging civil society. In essence, I pointed out that it was not surprising that President Reagan had serious misconceptions about the roles and capacities of voluntary organizations. Indeed, it was instructive that we had a president who was committed to strengthening voluntary initiative but ended up doing much the opposite. Though some attributed this to disingenuousness, it was more likely a result of a genuine misunderstanding of what voluntary organizations can and cannot do.

The president did devote a good deal of attention to the activities of nonprofit groups, including honoring private sector initiative by individuals, associations, and corporations. To the extent that a society is what it venerates, Reagan's efforts in that area were very helpful. Those advantages, however, were more than counterbalanced by many of his administration's other actions, which undermined the ability of voluntary organizations to fulfill the larger role the president expected of them. The difficulties began with the basic misunderstanding of the size and role of the voluntary sector. The president pushed these groups to more responsibility than they could assimilate. As a result, many of them, particularly those dealing with the most vulnerable people, faced intolerable expectations and ended up with a good deal of undeserved guilt and blame.

From the start of that administration, I was struck by how little those who were attempting to foster philanthropy and voluntary action really understood it. Within months of the inauguration, I found myself working with White House staff and those newly involved with the President's Task Force on Private Initiatives, many of whom really believed that corporate philanthropy alone, which then totaled only $3 billion, a minuscule fraction of one percent of the federal budget, could take over support of programs utterly beyond anything that corporate philanthropy could ever achieve. There was a total lack of understanding of the size of private giving. Even after we agreed to disagree on what public programs were wasteful or useful, they were still thinking in terms of transferring dollar responsibilities to private giving that could never, ever be assimilated. These were not people who were trying to find an excuse to cut public programs, though obviously there were some of those; these officials genuinely believed that private philanthropy and voluntary organizations were far larger than they were.

The Reagan administration's second mistake involved an unintended but serious undercutting of the income of many voluntary organizations. More than one-third of the income of the voluntary sector is provided by government contracts with nonprofit groups to carry out legislated programs such as job training centers, homes for the aged, and research universities. A significant and disproportionate share of government's budget cuts came out of the income of its voluntary contractors. It's much easier to cut budgets of distant partners than to reduce departments and staff within one's own operation. Simultaneously, several changes in the 1986 Tax Act undercut the ability of many voluntary groups to keep up with prior rates of fundraising growth. For the first full year following the tax changes, the rate of increased giving by individuals dropped 50 percent, just as we had warned the administration. To compound the income problem, the Reagan administration, which had forced most nonprofits to scramble for new and higher levels of noncontributed and nongovernmental support, tried to tax previously exempt categories of income, such as fees, sales, and interest.

There were repeated instances of the Reagan administration's efforts to curb advocacy activities of voluntary organizations. Office of Management and Budget proposals would have stripped from voluntary organizations that receive any government funding almost all of their rights to engage simultaneously in representations before government. Also, proposed Internal Revenue Service regulations would have restricted greatly the advocacy rights of all tax-exempt organizations.

In the composite, the voluntary organizations that President Reagan wanted to help were in fact faced with increased expectations, decreased government support, an undercutting of their ability to raise new money, the prospect of new taxes, and a challenge to their advocacy role.

In every administration, at least beginning with President Nixon's and including those of both Democrats and Republicans, there have been serious proposals to strip altogether the nonprofit status of organizations that emphasize activism and advocacy. To describe one revealing and alarming example requires me to use the epitome of Washington jargon, for the episode involved something called "OMB A-122." In 1983, the Office of Management and Budget (OMB) proposed to change the conditions contained in Circular A-122, which governs many of the contractual relationships between the Federal government and voluntary organizations. Those changes would have stripped from voluntary organizations that receive any government funding almost all of their rights to simultaneously engage in advocacy or even representations before government. For example, if a local unit of Catholic Charities responded to a city's request to help administer a research project on improving family care and accepted even a small grant to carry out that function, that unit would have forfeited all rights to advise or criticize the government on any matter, even if it used its contributed income to do so. Though those regulations were substantially beaten back, much of the same intent and language has reappeared in several administrations and Congresses since.

There is a pervasive attitude within government that voluntary *service* is to be applauded and *advocacy* is to be disdained. This ignores the reality that much of the best voluntary effort in our history relates to those who advocated most of the public programs we take pride in today. Public officials will point with obvious delight to the influence of such crusaders as Jane Addams and Dorothea Dix, who broke the barriers of public indifference to excruciating human need, but the same officials tend to view as annoying, troublesome, and maybe even dangerous those who today advocate for inclusion of hospice coverage in Medicaid, or insist that state government cannot wash its hands of a schizophrenic who is discharged from a state mental hospital.

In part, this constant effort to limit citizen voices relates to where government comes down on the balance between liberty and order. It also relates to what the economist Joseph Schumpeter described more than fifty years ago as the inexorable drift of power toward government unless strong countervailing voices can at least slow it. Daniel Patrick Moynihan, speaking at the founding meeting of INDEPENDENT SECTOR, described that frightening prospect:

> I think many of you will remember reading Joseph Schumpeter's last great book [*Capitalism, Socialism and Democracy*] in which he

said how this wonderfully creative civilization which we have produced in North America and Western Europe is going to come to
an end—not in some great apocalyptic Armageddon in which one
class takes over another class and destroys all classes. No. It will
come to an end through the slow but steady conquest of the private
sector by the public sector.

There is nowhere that this is more in evidence and more advanced than with respect to the non-government enterprises of
public concern which you represent. Little by little, you are being
squeezed out of existence or slowly absorbed. . . . Your job is to as-
sert that something of the most profound concern to American society is at issue, and that is our tradition of a plural, democratic society. It would be the final irony if, in the name of good purposes,
government ended up destroying liberty in the society. But that can
happen, and that is what seems to me is your job to make certain
does not happen.[11]

At times, efforts to limit activities of citizen groups stem from
very conservative or liberal ideology. I recall, now with some
amusement, two instances that at the time were very scary. In the
Nixon administration, the head of ACTION, the government agency
responsible for working with voluntary organizations, proposed
crippling limitations on grassroots associations because in his view
they seriously interfered with community stability by undermin-
ing the status quo and the authority of the existing power structure. And in the Carter administration, the head of the same
agency wanted to use its power to challenge the existence of large
established institutions such as the Ford Foundation, the United
Way, and the Junior League because in his view they were neither
democratically based nor focused on grassroots constituencies and
causes—in other words, they were too reflective and protective of
the status quo and the existing power structure.

Some of my most trying times involved dealing with people
who insisted that government protect their freedom to do what
they passionately believed was in the public interest but who
wanted the same government to use its power to squelch those
with whom they bitterly disagreed. At one point when this pattern
became ludicrous bordering on frightening, I wrote a piece that
the *Christian Science Monitor* published as "Don't Save Me from
the Left or Right."

From two extremes, people who believe passionately in freedom are calling for increased regulations to restrict what their opposites can do.

With the growing influence of conservative evangelical churches, liberals are calling for revision of the laws that define what a religion is and what religions can't do. From their side, influential conservatives are promoting legal schemes to "defund the left," to limit the outreach of organizations like Planned Parenthood that deal with causes they consider dangerous to the country.

Liberals, who for fifty years have been listening to their Roman Catholic priests tell them how to vote, or who still hear their black preachers endorse candidates, or who encouraged their Lutheran ministers to march in Selma, want to clamp down on what can be done in the name of religion. Conservatives, who preach faith in people, minimal government, and clearer separation of church and state, want expansion of governmental control over what they define as unholy.

If both sides get their way, we'll have more laws to protect us from the right and the left—and less freedom for everyone.

Out of passion and bitterness, both sides are losing sight of the protection of the larger freedoms of speech and assembly, and of their wide-open opportunities to spread what they consider the truth. Any infringement of these freedoms and opportunities will sooner or later infringe both of them and all of us.

If some people believe that the rest of us must be protected from certain extreme ideas, or if they're frightened that we won't make the right decisions for ourselves, our families, and our communities, there is comfort in Thomas Jefferson's advice: "I know of no safe depository of the ultimate powers of society but the people themselves; and if we think them not enlightened enough to exercise their control with a wholesome discretion, the remedy is not to take it from them, but to inform their discretion by education."

Norman Lear started People for the American Way to warn people of the seductive media campaigns of the Moral Majority, and if Lear goes too far, someone else will come along to correct him. Along the way, the people learn and grow.

There are some causes in the land that I believe are downright dangerous, and there are situations where opposing crusades spend staggering amounts only to achieve a standoff. Our protection—

and theirs—is in our right to disclose what we know, not to fore-
close what they do.

If some groups clearly trespass the law, the authority is already
at hand to deal with them. Hopefully, though, the law will not be
administered with a heavy hand. Democracy and I can survive my
priest telling me how to vote on a candidate who supports federal
appropriations for abortions, but we will not survive if he can be
too easily silenced on public issues, or if true believers in any cause
can legally stifle their doubters.[12]

I'm often asked about "fringe groups" and how to distinguish
between "healthy and unhealthy organizations." These questions
are usually in the form of a challenge to any possible justification
for the existence of groups that they consider "fringe" such as various militia groups and cults.

Much of the activity people deplore is in fact already illegal and
should be prosecuted: organizations that infringe on the rights of
others, or are outright frauds, or provide more personal benefit to
the operators than public benefit to the advertised causes. Such
uncivil behavior should not be tolerated in a civil society. If that
kind of activity is pursued either by an informal or formal group,
those involved should be punished to the full extent of the law.
That includes any militia-like organizations and cults that
threaten or attack the lives or rights of others. For me, they're way
beyond even fringe.

Society's course becomes less clear for groups that are border-
line or that seem to go against what the majority might consider
acceptable behavior. Even here, most determinations have to be
left to personal choice or to law.

In my experience, the vast majority of citizen groups—probably as high as 99 percent—are respectable and try to do right by
the causes they embrace. However, to the extent that they have the
benefit of tax exemption and ask for public support, they have a
moral obligation to disclose their makeup, activities, and finances,
and I favor increased legal responsibility for just such openness. If
citizen groups put themselves above the law—or worse, if they
misbehave in the name of charity—they become a real threat to
public confidence. When public confidence erodes, public protections and support erode also.

The balance of liberty and order is determined by the degree to which people and their representatives support or deplore the democratic cacophony.

Frederick Douglass expressed it this way: "Those who profess to favor freedom, and yet deprecate agitation, are people who want crops without plowing the ground. They want the ocean without the awful roar of its many waters."[13] And Justice John Harlan interpreted it thus: "The constitutional right of free expression is powerful medicine in a society as diverse and populous as ours; that the air may at times seem filled with verbal cacophony is, in this sense, not a sign of weakness but of strength."[14]

Both the fragility of the balance between liberty and order and the concomitant need to define and protect the liberties legally were brought home to me in a consultation with leaders of Hong Kong's civil service shortly before the Chinese "takeover." I had become involved because some leaders of Hong Kong's NGO sector and some conscientious civil service leaders were concerned that there was little mention of nongovernmental activity in China's laws and that therefore after June 30, 1997, these organizations would be particularly vulnerable to arbitrary rulings on their right to exist and what they could and could not do.

In preparation for my visit, I did what checking was possible and found clear signs that Beijing and even the new Hong Kong government would emphasize responsibilities over rights and that groups critical of the government would be disbanded or muted. When I had an opportunity to ask a key person in the Hong Kong government whether provision would be made for the legal status and protection of nonprofit groups, he rushed to report that agreement had just been reached to allow such groups to register and that the conditions of approval were being worked out. Before he could move on to other points I asked him with whom the voluntary organizations would register and he cryptically replied that it would be the police.

Despite every indication that he was through with my line of questioning, I asked further whether the police could easily bar groups that criticize government policy. He said that they could, and should, because those groups would be trying to foment trouble if not rebellion. I interjected that I was talking not about groups advocating the overthrow of the government but about groups concerned about public policies or programs dealing with the environment or crippled children. The official cut me off by saying that such groups should seek more orderly ways to communicate with government.

Before he turned away altogether, I asked him if the groups that were allowed to register would be allowed to hold public meetings and he replied that perhaps so if they got prior approval. "I suppose," I asked, "it would be the police who would make that decision?"

"Of course," he said, with finality.

By the time I returned to the United States the announcement had been made that the new government would curb a range of civil rights including limits on public demonstrations and a requirement that all organizations register with the police.

The experience with Hong Kong underscored what I'd been learning repeatedly in my work with CIVICUS: that there can be little hope for citizen participation and influence or even protection of such fundamental rights as speech, assembly, and association, if the laws don't stipulate these rights and the courts don't protect them.

Groups around the world struggling for these basic rights assume that everything is secure in the United States, but INDEPENDENT SECTOR and others struggle with legislative and court challenges to those rights.

I devote about a third of *Powered by Coalition: The Story of* INDE-PENDENT SECTOR to such challenges and our ability to deal reasonably well with them. That ability came from our having finally achieved significant unity within this broad disparate nonprofit sector to marshal the case and the votes. In the chapter "Battles and Cooperation with Government," I pointed out that such issues, especially those that would have limited the necessary degree of independence for philanthropic and voluntary organizations, were never far from our top priorities.

Over the fifteen years of my active leadership of the organization, there were eleven very serious proposals to limit the rights of organizations; they came at us from many different directions. In 1993 alone, there were seven serious legislative and regulatory proposals that would have dangerously limited the advocacy rights of voluntary organizations and their funders. Successful efforts to defeat those threats took every speck of effort by every part of the organization, but in the end we were able to prevail. Doing so meant protection of the sector's quintessential role in providing the organizational vehicles through which citizens express their concerns and ideas.[15]

Also in the INDEPENDENT SECTOR story, I reported that among the most significant examples of our shared achievements were the Supreme Court cases involving the freedoms of speech and assembly. The organizing committee had made it clear that the highest of all the many priorities was to address "the fundamental relationship between the freedom of citizens to organize themselves and the freedom of citizens."[16]

That was our orientation and motivation for diving into the Supreme Court case *Village of Schaumburg v. Citizens for a Better Environment et al.* in 1979, even before INDEPENDENT SECTOR was fully formed and before we had anything like the resources or experience to justify an all-out defense of associational freedoms. Schaumburg had established a limit of 25 percent on fund-raising costs for organizations applying for a permit to solicit support in that community. We recognized that unpopular and newer causes might exceed that limit, at least in early years of operation, and that therefore communities could use the fund-raising limit to squelch their critics. We argued for full disclosure but not foreclosure.

We were deeply involved, in our early years, with other Supreme Court cases that could have weakened essential freedoms. Fortunately we prevailed, and these victories strengthened further the capacity of voluntary organizations to be a means by which citizens express and exercise collective will. Writing in celebration of those judicial successes, I emphasized both the rights that had been protected and the responsibility we had be worthy of those rights:

> Organizations of this sector operate with funds voluntarily contributed and therefore have the highest moral responsibility to be absolutely certain that we fulfill the public's trust. We also enjoy the advantages of tax exemption and therefore have particular responsibility to cooperate with government in developing sound oversight laws and compliance with them. There is nothing less attractive in our society than people who cheat and defraud in the name of charity. . . . We and government have a mutual responsibility to

establish appropriate expectations. In doing so, however, neither of us should ever be allowed to become so judgmental that we obscure the quintessential role of this sector to protect and encourage maximum citizen interest and participation. In that regard, we are right to rejoice in and celebrate this additional Supreme Court protection of freedom of speech.[17]

At times, the threats to organizational and personal freedoms were painfully real. One prolonged nightmare involved White House efforts to squelch its critics. For me and for many in the sector, this chilling episode started as far back as the early 1970s, when I was the national director of the Mental Health Association (MHA). In 1972, the MHA celebrated victories in Congress that took the form of greatly increased appropriations for mental health research, training, and community treatment. Those new appropriations amounted to approximately $125 million per year, to be awarded by the federal government to state and local mental health authorities, *not* including the association itself. For an organization that was raising about $25 million a year, those were major accomplishments.

After succeeding in getting the legislation passed and then the funds appropriated and authorized, we were horrified that President Nixon "impounded" the money in a demonstration of his antagonism toward the subject and field of mental illness/mental health. We were absolutely stymied, because Congress, having already approved the funds, had no further role. It was a standoff between those two branches of government, with only the Supreme Court left as possible arbiter. Our feisty group, struggling with the unpopular cause of mental illness, sued the president of the United States, and in two separate cases our issues careened their way to the Supreme Court, where eventually we won both, and on lopsided votes. It was one of the greatest victories ever for the MHA.

Not long after the Supreme Court's decisions, some of our MHA state affiliates became the subject of financial and program audits. I knew what a financial audit was, but I had never heard of a program audit. I learned quickly that it entailed an examination of whether we were exceeding the amount of advocacy effort allowed by what was then a very indefinite formula. At that stage, our state affiliates were trying to improve conditions relating to state mental hospitals, rehabilitation programs, and the like. It was pretty obvious that the best affiliates would be heavily involved in influencing public policies and programs. Thus, we were highly vulnerable to a claim that we exceeded the "insubstantial" amount of resources that could be expended for advocacy.

At about that time, I was told by both government insiders and informed observers that I was on the so-called enemies list of the Nixon White House. I never knew if that was really so, or even if there was such a list, but I soon had no doubt that somebody high up was indeed out to get us, and was using the IRS to do so. On the personal side, they couldn't do very much because my tax returns were pretty simple. It was the only time in my life I was relieved and grateful to have so little money!

For the organization, the consequences were becoming horrific. One after the other, our state affiliates were reporting that IRS auditing teams were showing up, focusing little attention on financial records, and giving painstaking scrutiny to minutes, correspondence, and anything else that could provide a sense of interactions with government. Within months, we learned that our enormously effective Maryland division would lose its tax exemption, and it looked as if others would too.

We thought we might get relief by using an old contact with the current IRS commissioner, but he angrily rejected any notion that his organization was politicized. Years later, I learned that in fact he was unaware that White House officials had gained considerable leverage over key people in the IRS, particularly with respect to so-called enemies.

In desperation, we turned to influential members of Congress, who fortunately understood that the administration's arbitrary interpretation of "substantial" or "insubstantial" left us at the mercy of federal officials who might object to our efforts to influence them. Congressman Barber Conable and Senator Edmund Muskie took up our cause, and with their help we were able to enlist impressive cosponsors of legislation that would specify what legislative activity was appropriate for voluntary groups and even declare that advocacy was healthy in the development of sound public policies and programs. The legislators made their displeasure clear to the IRS and the White House and demanded that during consideration of the legislation, foreclosures of tax exemption should be limited to cases of egregious behavior.

After two years of growing support and negotiation, Congress finally passed the law "Lobbying by Public Charities," which clarified and expanded the lobbying rights of nonprofit groups. With our new law on the books, the MHA was free of retaliatory efforts, though in certain IRS regions, arbitrary interpretations of the law were somewhat difficult to counter because the related tax regulations were slow in coming.

Actually, "slow in coming" is hardly an accurate description. It was ten years before the IRS got around to issuing proposed regulations, and when these finally surfaced, they were brutal in their prohibitions and inhibitions. Contrary to the statute to which they related, which made clear through word and legislative history that advocacy was to be encouraged within broad limits, the regulations treated advocacy as egregious and punishable.

By 1986, I was serving as president of INDEPENDENT SECTOR, but had quite naturally remained interested in the prospective regulations. However, I had not really focused on them until all sorts of people who knew nothing about my MHA background began to tell me of rumors of the awful regulations soon to be issued by the IRS. *Déjà vu* was never more poignant or painful.

Beginning with an optional session of INDEPENDENT SECTOR members in late December 1986 to compare information and develop strategy, I was back in the thick of it again. INDEPENDENT SECTOR was immediately up to its ears in desperate efforts to protect hundreds of thousands of organizations from perverse IRS interpretation of advocacy rights. My notes indicate that INDEPENDENT SECTOR spent considerable time on this issue at every board meeting between January 1987 and September 1990—almost four years! Because the INDEPENDENT SECTOR nationwide network was by then in place, we were able to create a firestorm of protest, including many examples of specific and horrendous implications for people and causes in almost every congressional district.

Lawrence Gibbs, a relatively new IRS commissioner, was at first totally supportive of his staff but couldn't help being bewildered by the sheer number of respected organizations and people, including former commissioners, leaders of Congress, and many others, who argued for reexamination. At our instigation, the majority of the House Ways and Means Committee, the Senate Finance Committee, and the House Appropriations Committee signed letters to Gibbs urging withdrawal. It didn't take him long to compare the original legislation with the regulations and realize that someone was looking at the two very differently. It would have been awkward for a commissioner to withdraw proposed regulations; instead, Gibbs issued a news release that said the proposals would be reexamined.

At that point, the commissioner asked me to bring a group of leaders to see him so that he could get a firsthand sense of the issues and of those who were leading a campaign upsetting to his leadership and organization. I think he found it unbelievable that we behaved like intelligent, rational human beings who didn't carry placards and spears. I explained our grievances and, with Thomas Troyer of the law firm Caplin and Drysdale, presented a comparison of the origins of the 1976 legislation, the legislation itself, and the contradictory regulations. Then, representatives of various parts of the sector, such as arts, human rights, and education, explained why they found the regulations so inappropriate to their public service roles.

Not long after that session, there was a second gathering, which brought together a delegation from INDEPENDENT SECTOR and many of the IRS staffers who had been involved in developing the regulations. Any observer would have concluded that it was not a very successful beginning to the resolution of different perceptions and mutual distrust. At one point, someone on our side pointed out that the regulations were bad enough, but would lead to even more exaggerated interpretations by auditors in the IRS regions responsible for compliance. With that, we were taken to task with the reminder that the IRS was above political influence and so rigidly objective and professional that it was an insult to suggest that prejudice or worse could enter into future reviews.

I tried as politely as possible to describe my Mental Health Association experience, in order to demonstrate that, in my case at least, the IRS had behaved in the worst possible way, leading me to distrust personal assurances that the regulations would be administered fairly. Despite my efforts to be reasonably calm and quietly truthful, it was obvious that the IRS staffers were startled, disbelieving, and angry. In essence, the session involved our questioning their objectivity, fairness, and—worse—their professionalism. It didn't go well, and except for an agreement to meet again, it didn't end well.

Within a couple of days, I received a call from a key figure in the IRS, who said he had been instructed by even higher authority to call me to relay the Service's chagrin, acknowledgment, and apologies for what the records clearly revealed was grossly inappropriate behavior in the case involving the MHA's Maryland affiliate, and perhaps others. It was obviously a painful call for him to make, but he did it with dignity and kindness.

Shortly afterward, Gibbs accepted a suggestion we had made to establish an Exempt Organizations Advisory Group, made up primarily of leaders from our sector and legal and tax experts on philanthropic and voluntary organizations. For the next two years, discussions proceeded on two and then three levels, leading to the resolution of the immediate issue of the advocacy regulations and to the exploration of many other important matters relating to the IRS and nonprofits. The advisory group met regularly to learn of the progress of a working group on the regulations and, where necessary, to form new working groups on other matters. Gradually, there developed regular consultation between INDEPENDENT SECTOR and the IRS. As you might imagine, this required mutual respect and the ability to compromise and disagree. We had changed from absolute adversaries, to wary negotiators, to cooperative professionals earning and depending on each other's respect.

Lest that example of government misbehavior seem altogether isolated and rare, it has been my sad experience to face several very real threats of retaliation for being part of entirely legitimate efforts to convince or, if necessary, force government to obey its own laws.

A briefer but still chilling episode occurred within days of my becoming head of the National Council on Philanthropy (NCOP). It involved a visit with a delegation of badge-flashing intelligence agents who demanded, on the basis of a small grant NCOP had received from one of their organizations, that I include some of their people in our delegations to international meetings. When I refused, I was told that in a study of my record, it had come to light that as a sophomore in high school, I had been a member of the United World Federalists, which they implied could ruin my career.

I told them two things: one, I was proud of being a student member of that idealistic organization, about which I had never seen or heard a hint of unpatriotic behavior (indeed always the opposite); and two, I had been enlisted into that group by a famous badly wounded Marine officer whose career I had followed and who was at that point the second or third highest official in the CIA. I never heard another threatening word.

If such experiences could happen to a generally moderate change maker like myself, then the tales are not exaggerated for what happens to those raising a ruckus in such controversial areas as civil rights or control of nuclear power. I have become a true believer in Lord Acton's conclusion that "power corrupts and absolute power corrupts absolutely"; and I believe all the more in Alexander Hamilton's dictum that "the price of liberty is eternal vigilance."

James Luther Adams reminds us of the stark reality of how quickly Germany lost its freedom.

> One of the first things Adolf Hitler did after seizing power was to abolish, or attempt to abolish, all organizations that would not submit to control. The middle organizations—for example, the universities, the churches, and voluntary associations—were so lacking in political concern that they created a space into which a powerful charismatic leader could march with his Brown Shirts. . . . This toboggan slide into totalitarianism was accelerated by the compliance of governmental structures, provincial and local, including the secondary school system. Considering this broad range of compliance, we may define the totalitarian society as one lacking effective mediating structures that protect the self-determination of individuals and groups.[18]

In a *Washington Post* opinion piece, Henry Owen, then director of foreign policy studies at the Brookings Institution, summarized his view of the Holocaust.

> The Holocaust was mainly the Nazis' fault, but we miss the central point if we think of it as being solely their responsibility. The Holocaust has more to tell us than that. It tells us that Jacob Burckhardt, the Swiss historian, and Lord Acton were right when they wrote, amid the general optimism of the 19th century, that the combination of continued human imperfection and growing human power was an increasingly dangerous one. It was the work not only of the instigators but of an entire generation which, when faced with evil, for the most part did nothing. It was the work of a

generation, of Germans and others, who had been too busy or ambitious or clever to pay much attention to anything except being good architects, good businessmen, good engineers, or what have you.[19]

Francis Fukuyama provides other riveting examples of the collapse of civil society:

> [Gellner's] Conditions of Liberty gives much support to the view that civil society is something much easier for the state to destroy than to construct. Besides the Communist examples it discusses, there are many cases of overly strong and ambitious centralized states undercutting the ability of societies to organize themselves in intermediate associations. From the Chinese imperial system to the Norman kingdom in southern Italy to the French monarchy in the sixteenth and seventeenth centuries, pre-modern rulers have gutted their respective civil societies and left populations unable to cohere on the basis of anything other than kinship groups or formal, state-sponsored organizations. Once having been established, these patterns have persisted for centuries afterwards—suggesting that the regeneration of civil society may never happen in certain former Communist countries.[20]

Other serious threats to civil society have been covered earlier but two should be repeated here: the increasing division between rich and poor and the pattern of campaign financing that makes elected officials more responsive to special interests than to constituents.

Getting a handle on the *state* of civil society is compounded by more than just its limitations and threatened circumstances. It's complicated also by a wide range of often firmly held opinions about the state of our society, the effectiveness and usefulness of our government, and whether anything can be done to turn the public around.

Some views and the publicity they seem to attract and spread, make it particularly hard to be objective and hopeful. Stephen C. Craig even titles his book *Malevolent Leaders: Popular Discontent in America*, and says, "We know for a fact that Americans have been mad as hell for quite a few years. What remains to be seen is whether they're prepared to let their leaders know that they refuse to take it anymore."[21]

The publisher of Georgie Anne Geyer's book *Americans No More: The Death of Citizenship* describes her message as, "Citizenship in the United States has changed drastically and for the worse."[22] Daniel Yankelovich begins a *Kettering Review* article, "The American public is in a foul mood. People are frustrated and angry. They are anxious and off balance. They are pessimistic about the future and cynical about all forms of leadership and government."[23] Robert D. Putnam writes ominously of "the strange disappearance of social capital in America" defining social capital as "features of social life—networks, norms, and trust—that enable participants to act together more effectively to pursue shared objectives."[24] These and other concerns support the common view that confidence in our society is low and sinking.

I think I know the concerns and problems about as well as anyone, but I don't come out of the appraisal nearly so pessimistic or frightened. I don't think we are in a free fall. I even see signs that the trends are slowly improving. Indeed we can find more balanced views of the state of our democracy and its essential underpinnings in civil society by reading further into the writings of those who get our attention with visions of collapse. For example, Yankelovich ends his piece: "Only a powerful political will can overcome these immense difficulties. But I believe that the potential for mobilizing such a political will exists in the nation today."[25] Writers such as Craig and Geyer whose book titles raise the specter of "malevolent leaders" and "the death of citizenship," conclude with hopeful outlooks and agendas. So, even many of those who would scare the public the most, and unfortunately succeed, balance their pessimism with hope rarely captured in the sound bites.

Some observers and writers begin with more optimistic outlooks. For example, the American Association of Retired Persons recently released a report conducted by the Center for Survey Research of the University of Virginia which, according to David Broder, indicates:

America is more of a society of "joiners" than Putnam and many other earlier scholars had calculated. . . . the AARP study found that the average American adult has four affiliations. Only one in seven has no formal links outside the family or work. . . . the survey advances the understanding of the state of civic life more than any other study I have ever read.[26]

In contrast to the tone of Geyer's subtitle, *The Death of Citizenship*, Alan Wolfe has titled a book *One Nation, After All* summarizing his study of "middle class morality" and concluding: "By combining traditional ideals with modern realities, even if in ways discordant to intellectuals and ideologues, [our] middle-class morality offers the best formula for making the United States the one nation economically it already is morally."[27] Putnam's alarming diagnosis of the state of our social capital is countered by several very different interpretations, such as Everett C. Ladd's "A Vast Empirical Record Refutes the Idea of Civic Decline"[28] and Robert J. Samuelson's column " 'Bowling Alone' Is Bunk."[29]

With clear evidence that a sizable part of the population is concerned, angry, or indifferent, we have to be more precise about their concerns, the specific problems underlying them, and the negativism and discouragement that stand in the way of mobilizing for solutions.

A Charles Stewart Mott Foundation report headed "America's Tattered Tapestry" provides examples of the crushing concerns that cause many to feel helpless and threatened.

- fear that we are a nation devoid of values;
- fear that the family, as we know it, is collapsing;
- fear that the children of our inner cities won't live to see their 20s;
- fear that our promise is lost and that our children will never enjoy a standard of living equal to our own;
- fear that our systems of education, government and medical care can't meet the needs of today, let alone tomorrow;
- fear that the jobs and pensions of today will be gone tomorrow;
- fear that there is no way out of the despair and hopelessness brought about by persistent poverty;
- fear of competing cultures;
- fear of each other; and
- fear that no one really cares.[30]

John Gardner covers his own list of "grim problems," adding insights into the negative social and political realities that thwart optimism and progress:

> The arena of national politics is dispiriting. Pit bull partisanship. The sleight-of-hand of the image manipulators. Politicians walking the tightrope over an angry electorate.
>
> The problems are frightening but in themselves are not as perplexing as the questions they raise concerning our capacity to gather our forces and act. The prevailing mood is cynicism. To mobilize the required resources and bear the necessary sacrifices calls for a high level of motivation. Is it possible that our shared values have disintegrated to the point that we can no longer lend ourselves to any worthy common purpose?[31]

In the early 1990s the National Civic League, in conjunction with the Gallup International Institute, conducted a survey of the public's thoughts about the state of their communities and their own participation. The results add context to the problems and the question of who should be responsible for them. More than 97 percent said their communities faced a major problem(s) and the top four concerns were the economy (23 percent), drugs (16 percent), crime (9 percent), and environmental issues (8 percent). However, only 23 percent indicated confidence in their local municipal government and 20 percent in their state government to deal with their local issues.[32]

A later and recently updated study by the Harwood Group for the Kettering Foundation headed "Citizens and Politics: A View from Main Street America" included among its principal findings:

> Americans are frustrated about politics—at a depth not previously revealed—and feel pushed out of the whole process. "Many Americans don't believe they are living in a democracy," says Kettering President David Mathews. "They describe the present political system as impervious to public direction."[33]

The Kennedy School of Government at Harvard has undertaken a multi-year project, "Visions of Government for the Twenty-First Century," which began with an analysis called "Why People Don't Trust Government." In the introduction of the book of the same title, Joseph S. Nye, Jr., sets out some of the concerns the school uncovered:

> Confidence in government has declined. In 1964, three-quarters of the American public said that they trusted the federal government to do the right thing most of the time. Today only a quarter of Americans admit to such trust. The numbers are only slightly better—35 percent—for state government. Some polls show even lower levels. A 1995 poll showed a confidence rate of 15 percent at the federal level, 23 percent at the state level, and 31 percent at the local level. In 1997, the same poll showed a slight improvement to 22, 32, and 38 percent at the federal, state, and local levels, still far behind the numbers three decades ago. The top reasons given for distrusting government are that it is inefficient, wastes money, and spends on the wrong things.[34]

Nye and his coauthors provide helpful balance to that disturbing information by indicating for example that "the public overwhelmingly thinks the United States is the best place to live [80 percent] and we like our democratic system of government [90 percent]." Nye observes, "something is steady."[35]

The American public's sorry performance on voting is the most often cited indication of lack of participation and abrogation of responsibility. Though many have tried to figure out why so many of us don't vote, I haven't come across any report that pins it down or provides a solution to turn it around. To be sure that the facts at least are in perspective, our performance looks like this: In 1996, 62 percent of those eligible were registered to vote and 40 percent actually voted in federal elections. In 1960, the figures were 70 percent and 60 percent, respectively.[36]

A 1982 report from The New World Foundation indicated that "non-voters are a nation larger than France in our midst. And of all the nations using the ballot, only Botswana has a voter turnout rate lower than the United States."[37] The report included information from the Committee for the Study of the American Electorate, which identified five major problems in our political system that might help explain voter apathy:

1. There no longer exists a national consensus about what's worth doing and how to go about it.

2. Leadership is ineffective in dealing with major social and economic challenges.

3. Decay of the political parties means there's no longer a disciplined way to coordinate collective action and even if policies did exist—no way to deliver.

4. Decline in social institutions, increasing anomie and atomization, have encouraged a narrowing of self-interest.

5. TV has removed a sense of history from politics and elevated personalities to the point where "elections become a circus."[38]

The studies and experiments on voting multiply, which is a good sign, though the absence of solutions is still a dangerous sign.

In the Civic League's report indicating lack of confidence in government, there were also these findings:

Churches and local community organizations are seen as the institutions best able to deal with community problems.

Almost 30 percent indicated that they are now involved with community problems or would like to be.

Those who are now involved give most of their time to religious-based organizations, youth groups, education, health care, and senior citizens.[39]

In discussing the independent sector, I pointed out the burgeoning of voluntary action throughout our society and the impact these volunteers and their organizations are achieving. People believe they can make a difference through volunteer service.

The analogy about the glass being half empty or half full probably never fit a situation more exactly than that of volunteering. For about fifteen years, INDEPENDENT SECTOR's surveys of volunteering have shown that approximately half the adult population volunteers and at an average of four hours a week. On the other hand, the other half of the population can't remember doing anything for anybody last week, last month, or last year. While not unconcerned about the latter half, I've always focused on those who are generous. From what we know of the situation in other countries, our degree of participation is extraordinary.

Even for the other half, those who seem too self centered to help others, there are hopeful signs. Hodgkinson's research indicates that those who seem so heartless or selfish have very much the same values as those who do participate and indeed they respect and envy those who are active. Thus, we're up against, not 50 percent of the population who wouldn't dream of getting involved, but the challenge of finding ways to help these individuals get involved.

In the Kettering/Harwood survey revealing negative attitudes toward government, other findings showed people's distinct willingness to help others and their desire to strengthen government. "Civic duty is far from dead," the survey reported. "Citizens are still actively participating in public life, but on a local level where they believe they can make a difference—and they're not calling their civic actions 'politics.' "[40]

Despite my faith in voluntary institutions, I don't view it as healthy that people favor this sector, particularly if that attitude is used as a reason for neglecting government. Ingram and Smith indicate that increased emphasis on nongovernmental public service could detract from participation in politics.[41]

When pressed, most of us are likely to agree that "somebody ought to do something" and we probably assume that the somebody is someone other than ourselves. Most often we expect we can just leave it to citizens generally or government specifically even while our confidence in government wanes and our participation in it deteriorates.

In "Public Space for a Civil Society in Eclipse," published in *Kettering Review*, Benjamin R. Barber speaks about the dilemma of solving our largest problems if the people are not involved with public policy: "The question of how America's compound, decentralized multivocal public can secure a coherent voice in debates over public policy remains one of the thorniest both in American social science and in the practice of democratic politics."[42]

The Kennedy School study suggests that the solutions may begin with a clearer understanding of the public's concerns, fuller facts about the shortcomings of government, and a better grasp of what citizens can do about their concerns, including making communities and government more effective. The project provides fascinating examples of how far off the mark some of our impressions and even some of our largest concerns turn out to be. Derek Bok, in "Measuring the Performance of Government," reports on a series of extreme misperceptions, such as "most people estimate that more than 50 cents of every dollar in the social security program is eaten up in overhead. The true figure is less than 2 cents."[43] Bok reports on more than seventy-five "specific objectives of importance to most Americans" (such as the economy, housing, and percent of people graduating from high school), and he concludes that despite the public's assumptions to the contrary, "the United States has made definite progress over the past few decades in the vast majority of [the seventy-five] cases."[44]

Though the public is frequently and naturally ambivalent about government and in recent times the frustrations and upsets have become enormous, the public is still proud of its democracy, eager to strengthen it, and willing to be of public service in many ways.

Chapter 4's coverage of effective citizenship gave many indications that individuals, voluntary organizations, and funders are interested in strengthening communities and civic effectiveness. It is also encouraging that most people are not turned off to all forms of participation.

For some and perhaps many of the people who are disillusioned, angry, and even frightened, their concerns might be eased by gaining a better perspective on the issues. A great many Americans, for example, are alarmed about the changing makeup of the U.S. population, particularly the new waves of refugees and immigrants. Though the problems are real, it's helpful to realize that most of us descend from people who were in the same circumstances, and that much of the strength of America stems from the values of immigrants, including hard work, belief in education, and the practice of religion. In "The Seeds of Urban Renewal," Michael Sviridoff writes eloquently about the positive side of our current population mix: "Masses of new people arrive each day, uplifting forsaken neighborhoods in ways beyond the expectation of earlier and failed urban redevelopment. They demonstrate, as did the older migrations, that new people possessed of a sturdy work ethic and stable families matter more than buildings."[45]

Another example in which understanding may ease concern relates to the so-called common values that so many people seem to espouse. A hard look at the issue reveals that a great problem involves whose and what values the various proponents would have us embrace. Many of those who plead for and even insist on a return to common beliefs and behavior in worship, patriotism, and togetherness hold rigidly to their own perception of those values and are intolerant of any deviation. Alex Comfort portrayed starkly the dark side of that proposition in his poem "The Song of Lazarus": "Remember when you hear them beginning to say Freedom. / Look carefully—see whose freedoms it is that they want you to butcher."[46]

Wolfe's study, *One Nation, After All*, referred to earlier, indicates that Americans still hold to the same basic values and accept that we all must be involved in achieving civility, including respecting differences in the way people look, speak, and worship. Gardner aptly calls this attitude "wholeness incorporating diversity."[47]

Even the terror of crime, which surveys tell us is the gravest worry of the most people, is yielding to evidence that citizen outrage and action can turn the tide. People are taking back their neighborhoods and growing more aware that failure to confront crime and such attendant issues as drugs and poverty is no longer tolerable for anybody.

The central point is that the problems that frustrate, frighten, or distance citizens are the responsibility of citizens to address, and the evidence is increasingly clear that, when citizens get involved and *organized*, progress occurs.

To prepare for a discussion of what we must do to improve the state of our personal and communal lives, it might be helpful to consider the rallying cry of the old civic warrior John Gardner:

> People want meaning in their lives; but in this turbulent era a context of meaning is rarely handed to us as a comfortable inheritance. Today we have to build meaning into our lives, and we build it through our commitments. One such commitment is service to one's community. And in a day when so many conscientious citizens actively avoid public life, it is worth adding that running for and serving in elective office is an honorable and courageous commitment.
>
> Let's tell people that there is hope. Let's tell them there's a role for everyone. We can save family and the children. We know how. We can demand and get accountable government. We can counter the mean-spirited divisiveness that undermines positive action. We can regenerate our shared values. We can release human talent and energy, and renew our institutions.

Now is the time to reach within ourselves, each to his or her own deepest reservoirs of faith and hope. Let's say to everyone who will listen:

"Lend a hand—out of concern for your community, out of love for our country, out of the depths of whatever faith you hold. Lend a hand."[48]

7

Preserving and Strengthening Civil Society

Freedom is participation in power.

CICERO

Whether one is pessimistic or optimistic about the state of democracy and its underpinnings in civil society, it is essential to strengthen them. Jean Bethke Elshtain and others suggest that the rallying point may be a new social covenant:

> If the great Roman republican citizen Cicero lamented that "we have lost the res publica," I bemoan the loss of something similar, the public citizen, and I embrace, as an alternative, a new social covenant in which we reach out once more to our fellow citizens from a stance of goodwill and work to defuse our discontents, so we might forge working alliances across various groups. Then and only then, I suggest, can we reclaim the great name *citizen*. For *citizen* is the name we give to our public identities and actions in a democratic society.[1]

I don't believe that it will be one particular spark or issue that leads to change but rather the general and growing discontent and a corresponding resolve to solve our problems. I also believe that the relatively quiet revolution is already occurring. As I move around the country and as I read about where leadership efforts are originating, I find that reform is already underway and is primarily of grassroots origin and force.

I've tried to put together, not a covenant or contract, but at least an action agenda that might take advantage of the concerns and crises and the many encouraging responses to them. It is what I think must be done if we are to succeed where the Athenians failed.

1. Bring into every level of formal education a preparation for citizenship and an understanding of the essential role of civil society in preserving and strengthening American democracy.

"The civic mission of American education" is the formal dedication of the book *Civitas: A Framework for Civic Education*.

> We believe that education for citizenship is the primary reason for establishing universal education in the American republic; i.e. the purpose to develop among all students, whether in private or in public schools, the virtues, sentiments, knowledge, and skills of good citizenship.[2]

In the foreword to *Higher Education and the Practice of Democratic Politics: A Political Education Reader,* David Mathews, discussing the origins of his book, proposes a similar goal.

> Over five years ago, a small informal group of faculty, administrators and students from a wide range of institutions began meeting to discuss a common concern with the way academia is educating young people for political responsibility, civic competence, and public leadership. . . .
>   In the sum, if colleges and universities are responsible for the development of the minds of their students, then they are certainly responsible for those particular modes of rationality that are civic. And if the civic affairs (politics) involve more than influencing governments, then that responsibility requires a reconsideration of even our best efforts to prepare the next generation for public life.[3]

In the past ten to fifteen years, considerable progress has been made to bring these topics into formal study. More than six hundred colleges and universities are now part of Campus Compact, which requires demonstrated commitment on the part of the institutions and direct involvement of their presidents "to help students develop the values and skills of citizenship through participation in public and community service."[4] Tufts University is a member of the compact and has even revamped its own mission to indicate that the very definition of a Tufts education includes preparation for a lifetime of service to society.

Close to fifty colleges have created academic centers devoted to civil society generally or major aspects of it such as philanthropy. The comprehensive centers are committed to stimulating related research throughout their institutions, increasing course offerings, providing an opportunity for students to be engaged in community service, and offering graduate education.

At the elementary and high school levels, a growing number of communities provide and encourage volunteer assignments and intellectual opportunities in the classroom to understand what all the participation means to the quality of society. Community Service Learning (CSL) is the umbrella concept that has come to describe the dual roles. It's described as "a method of teaching that promotes caring, contributing citizens; makes abstract knowledge relevant; engages the community in teaching efforts; and effects real community change."[5]

In *Hope and History*, Vincent Harding says that to succeed with students one must start with the teachers. In his chapter "Is America Possible?" Harding summarizes his own hopeful view: "The message is for all of us who teach. We are the nurturers, the encouragers of all the dreams, all the seeds deep in all the hearts where the future of a redeemed and rescued land now dwells."[6]

2. Accept civic literacy as a national priority for all Americans, including an understanding of the direct relationship between effective societies and the degree to which citizens can be and are active and influential.

The concept of lifelong learning was never better suited than in its application to citizenship. David Mathews urges attention to "educating for public life":

> Educating the civic self takes on new meaning when the public is recognized for what it really is. Civic literacy, the capacity of people

to think about the whole of things, of consequences and potential, becomes education of the most crucial kind. Public policy education becomes imperative in light of what the public can and must do; indeed what it alone can do.[7]

The new communication technologies such as TV and the Internet represent an enormous opportunity to advance civic literacy. The challenge will be whether we allow them to dumb down our minds and behavior or lift up our personal and public capacities for growth and quality of life. Walter B. Wriston, writing in *Foreign Affairs*, is very specific about the social possibilities of new communication technologies. In "Bits, Bytes, and Diplomacy," he writes: "Instead of validating Orwell's vision of Big Brother watching the citizen, the third revolution enables the citizen to watch Big Brother."[8]

In another overview of the blur of electronic change overtaking us and the possibilities of mastering it for social purposes, Lawrence K. Grossman, in his book *The Electronic Republic: Reshaping Democracy in the Information Age,* calls for non-commercial radio and television to be "converted into a vigorous independent well supported local and national interactive public telecommunications system."[9]

In a related speech to the National Academy of Public Administration, Grossman provided the striking example of the use of technology in the battle to ban land mines. He points to the recent co-winner of the Nobel Peace Prize, Jody Williams, and what she accomplished through technology. He indicates that less than three years ago, with no staff, no office, no membership, and just about no money, she combined her passion with a computer, the Internet, and a worldwide army of agitators and reformers and forced the recent treaty banning land mines.[10]

Robert Putnam, in "Tuning In, Tuning Out," concludes that our greatest obstacle in educating and activating people for involvement is the public's preoccupation with TV. He concludes, "The culprit is television," and argues that TV is damaging to social capital because of "time displacement . . . effects on the outlook of viewers . . . [and] effects on children."[11]

My message is not that the wizardry of communications can do it all; Wriston reminds us that it has to start with human will.

But despite all the advances of science and the ways in which it is changing the world, science does not remake the human mind or alter the power of the human spirit. There is still no substitute for courage and leadership in confronting the new problems and opportunities that our world presents.[12]

The notion and practice of "civic journalism" is gaining headway, though not without criticism. Essentially, the idea is to ask commercial media to devote more of their time and space to helping the public understand and deal with the major issues facing their communities. Mark Jurkowitz in a *Boston Globe* story described it as "news outlets . . . working with public-minded citizens to try to set a civic agenda." He wrote that, "In many cases, journalists become active partners in the search for solutions to community problems ranging from violent crime to downtown development. The hope is that, in recognition of all this effort, the politicians will pay attention."[13] Jay Rosen, director of the Project on Public Life and the Press at New York University, noted that the development of civic journalism is "nothing less than a 'classic American reform movement' designed to revitalize a dysfunctional democracy suffering from a disenfranchised citizenry and the cynical press."[14]

The idea is not without critics, particularly from those in the media who believe their job is to report the news, not make it. Having read a good bit on both sides, I come down on the side of reform. It comes back to my view that all institutions in this free land bear responsibility to be sure that democracy survives and thrives.

In our efforts to motivate citizens, it will help us to listen to the storytellers who remind us of our precious heritage and sacred trust. Their tales deepen our memory and stir us with pride and resolve. Vincent Harding says they are our "weavers of faith."[15] A favorite reminder for me to keep the dream alive is Ralph Waldo Emerson's poem for the dedication of the monument to the Minutemen who took their stand at Concord Bridge.

> By the rude bridge that arched the flood,
> Their flag to April's breeze unfurled,
> Here once the embattled farmers stood
> And fired the shot heard round the world.

The foe long since in silence slept;
Alike the conqueror silent sleeps;
And Time the ruined bridge has swept
Down the dark stream which seaward creeps.

On this green bank, by this soft stream,
We set to-day a votive stone;
That memory may their deed redeem,
When, like our sires, our sons are gone.

Spirit, that made those heroes dare
To die and leave their children free,
Bid Time and Nature gently spare
The shaft we raise to them and thee.[16]

3. Understand better what it takes to pass to future generations the practice of responsible citizenship, and develop every means to ensure that we succeed in passing along the rights and responsibilities.

Initially, I thought this concept would be included in the formal education category, but as I thought of my own experience and applied my own worries about the transfer, I decided it had to stand on its own. For one thing, I don't want to allow anyone to feel that the job belongs to someone else.

INDEPENDENT SECTOR and its former research director Virginia Hodgkinson have done some helpful studies that identify the factors most likely to assure that younger and future generations accept these essential obligations—including the obligation to pass them on to their successors. There are at least six primary factors that determine if a young person is likely to become an active citizen as an adult. Those factors are summarized in INDEPENDENT SECTOR's *Care and Community in Modern Society: Passing On the Tradition of Service to Future Generations.*[17] Essentially, young people grow up to be active participants if they:

1. Had parents or other adult role models who volunteered.
2. Were involved in a youth group or other voluntary organization.
3. Were involved in a religious congregation where they were

volunteers or were introduced to volunteer assignments outside
the congregation.
4. Were exposed to volunteering as part of school activity.
5. Saw respected young peers volunteer.
6. Were influenced by favorable media coverage of volunteering.

If all or most of these factors are present, a young person is almost certain to become an active community figure. For example,
if both parents volunteered, there is a 75 percent likelihood that
their children will become volunteers. Sixty percent will be volunteers if only one parent volunteered. Among children whose
parents did not volunteer, fewer than 40 percent will volunteer as
adults.[18]

Fortunately, several key influences are getting even stronger.
For example, many more schools are introducing students to volunteering and are adding classroom learning about what such service means to society. That activity is burgeoning from kindergarten through high school and into colleges.

Associations serving youth are also doing a great deal more to
encourage volunteering; the Boy Scouts and Girl Scouts, for example, have merit badges for community service. Also, some new
and increasingly influential organizations dedicated primarily to
youth service are enlarging the pool of younger volunteers, such
as the National Youth Leadership Council, Youth Service America, and AmeriCorps.

The central point is that we already know a great deal about
how to pass along habits of participation and responsibility and we
must organize ourselves to make sure the knowledge is put to
work. By spreading and strengthening the involvement of parents,
schools, congregations, youth-serving organizations, the media,
and others, we are likely to see the rewards for years and generations to come.

4. Expand and publicize research about what civil society is and its relationship to the protection and strengthening of democracy.

The whole book grows out of my concern for how little the public understands this "invisible colossus" and how little scholarly

and popular literature there is to improve our awareness and understanding.

In the Mott Foundation report, William White drew on important research produced by the Harwood Group to improve our understanding of the public's attitudes about government and democracy. He concluded from that study and subsequent consultations with many leaders that "the ground certainly seems fertile for a few carefully conceived, well executed experiments designed to reinvigorate democracy by re-engaging our citizenry."[19]

Various commissions, as we have seen, are at work on different aspects of civil society. The Ford Foundation has expanded significantly its own interest in the topic, including and initially emphasizing research. The Institute for a Civil Society, established in 1996, is "aimed at exploring and encouraging a civil society." In a front-page story in the *Boston Globe*, the president of that operation, Pam Solo, said, "everything we do is focused on supporting breakthroughs at the local level in strengthening and rebuilding a civil society."[20] The founding director of the Indiana Center on Philanthropy, Robert Payton, says that one of the most important priorities is "organized inquiry into the values, principles, and purposes of philanthropy, as well as efforts to better understand how our system works."[21] Virginia Hodgkinson's current work includes an analysis of the personal values that translate into caring behavior and community responsibility and how those values are learned.

If we really grasp how important citizen participation is, we must learn and apply all that can possibly be known about it.

5. Build on the sovereign role of citizens as the cornerstone of democracy.

David Mathews and many others argue for a return to the notion and practice of "citizens as the primary officeholders of government." He explains:

> Perhaps the worst way that professionalism perverts the axioms of professionals is in its presumption that citizens are like the people that professionals treat. Citizens are equated with consumers, patients, or readers. In all cases, these are largely passive roles . . . so

citizens—we the people who created the government—are reduced to government's clients.[22]

Stephen Craig, in discussing "Popular Discontent and the Future of Politics," says that, at the very least, citizens must make representative democracy work. Craig favors maximum citizen participation, but he believes it is in our vote that we exercise our greatest influence:

> What Americans want, in a nutshell, is to know that decision makers are capable . . . honest enough to resist the temptations that confront every politician sooner or later; dedicated to balancing the wishes of constituents with the needs of the larger community; flexible and willing to compromise in order to get things done but ready to stand on principle when the issue is one of right versus wrong; attentive to people's everyday concerns rather than to the selfish demands of special interest; and failing all else, truly accountable to voters at election time. . . . In the end, responsibility for closing the confidence gap rests mainly with the people themselves. . . .
> . . . Any restoration of trust depends upon the willingness of the politically inert rank and file to take seriously both the rights *and* the obligations of democratic citizenship, e.g., the obligations to be well informed, to participate, and to use one's vote to reward politicians who pursue the common good and punish those who do not.[23]

I acknowledged earlier that I'm hardly an expert on how to increase voting, but if there were a national resolve to do it, I believe we would somehow find a way. Maybe our problem is that we want to identify *the* impediment and devise *the* solution and want immediate results. But whatever the impediments, voting has to be the highest of our civic priorities. I know the experts differ on the importance of campaign finance reform, but common sense tells me that this has to rank pretty high in the battle plan.

Though voting is the primary way by which we influence politics, most of the others are also in poor shape. According to Harry C. Boyte in "Reinventing Citizenship":

> The decline of civic involvement in politics in recent years means that people lose a sense of their stake and ownership in the nation. They become outsiders and tourists of the age. The politics of seri-

ous democracy is the give-and-take, messy, everyday, public work through which citizens set about dealing with the problems of their common existence. Politics is the way people *become* citizens: accountable players and contributors to the country.[24]

When Boyte refers to our aversion to getting involved with *politics*—so often uttered with a combination of horror and disdain—it reminds me how often I hear people say that they *abhor* fundraising. Almost all of those who recoil from asking for money, though, are committed to their causes, whether better schools or a cure for cancer. I find I'm able to convince many people that asking for money for a cause they really believe in is not much more than explaining and articulating their passion to folks they talk to every day. I can't say that they end up loving fund-raising, but when they see it in this light they're no longer put off by it. I've had similarly favorable results with constituent contacts with their elected and appointed representatives, but because of the perceived mystique of the political system and the indefiniteness of results, it's harder to get people to engage in the governmental arena.

Maybe what we have to keep emphasizing is that the things people don't like about government are not going to get better until and unless *they* get engaged. The Kettering/Harwood report "Citizens and Politics" seems to suggest a way out of this contradiction or ambivalence.

Conventional wisdom seems to suggest that even if citizens were to sense the opportunity of political power, they would still find themselves too busy, too self-absorbed—"too everything"—to participate in public life. In other words, citizens are not willing to make the time to participate. This is essentially the argument that citizens are apathetic. But we have found that this is not the case: Americans do overcome these life-style obstacles when the right conditions exist. For instance, those citizens who identified the list of obstacles described above are the *very same* citizens who talked, often in eloquent and moving ways, about their involvement in meeting sundry public challenges in their own communities. Upon reflection, there was only one difference in the conditions that determined whether or not they ultimately acted. They were able to overcome the life-style obstacles before them when they believed that they *might* have an effect—that there was the possibility to create and witness change. It is this notion of *possibility* that is powerful in the realm of politics—and, especially, in reconnecting citizens and politics.[25]

To a significant extent, our ability to restore the concept and practice of citizens as the cornerstone of democratic government will depend on whether we can achieve reorientation of government and of the field of public administration to accept and foster maximum citizen participation and influence. People in government are as committed as other citizens to democracy and civil society, but they and the people who hold them accountable are not comfortable with maximum public involvement, particularly when they are being held accountable for coordinated, manageable, and efficient systems. Also, little in their selection and training prepares people in government for the high levels of ambiguity and conflict required by the democratic cacophony.

In their preface to *Public Policy and Democracy*, Ingram and Smith suggest that "public policy designed to foster democracy" is the ideal and primary goal of government.[26]

Elsewhere in this book I've dealt with threats to civil society, including a great many encroachments, both intentional and not, on the rights of voluntary organizations to be the vehicles for criticism and reform. One of my fondest hopes for this book is that it will help thoughtful legislators and other policymakers realize that democracy depends absolutely on a vibrant civil society, including an independent sector that is as independent as possible. The most important thing the government can do in this regard is to keep unobstructed the freedoms of religion, speech, and assembly, and such rights as petition and association.

6. Take fullest advantage of the new emphasis on community capacity building and community problem solving and apply what we already know about developing healthy neighborhoods, cities, and metropolitan regions.

Before proceeding in this necessary and appealing direction of community problem solving, I need to offer three cautions. The first is that although we seem to want less centralized government, we also want someone to be responsible and accountable for organizing the massive, often continent-wide crusades to deal with the seemingly endless lists of awful problems facing us. Even though we may be emotionally and intellectually committed to dispersion of authority and grassroots involvement, that commitment is challenged by day-to-day realities and our own conflicting desires. For example, we don't want one monolithic federal system for health care or social services, but we do stridently insist the systems that do exist are coordinated, comprehensive, and accountable. We don't want more federal government—except in the areas that we view as priority. If our priority is the criminal justice system, or cancer control, or clean air, or the rights of minorities or women, or learning disabilities, we can be exceedingly forceful in making the case that the federal government, as the representative of all the people, has a moral responsibility to deal with that priority. And the list is not limited to human suffering— witness the clamors about federal budgets for the National Endowment for the Arts.

Second, we need to do a far better job of sorting out which functions belong with what level of government and how we coordinate the many responsibilities that must be shared.

And third, as state and local governments transfer or share their expanded roles with nonprofit organizations and for-profit businesses, we are creating an even more dispersed system of services than the one we have and which is already the source of so much of our dissatisfaction about government ineffectiveness and the pluralistic hodgepodge that torments us. Long ago when I was at the Maxwell School of Citizenship and Public Affairs, our dean, Paul Appleby, said that our role was "to make a mesh of things." They didn't teach us how, and still don't, but if we are committed to decentralized and dispersed systems that must also be effective, manageable, and accountable, we had better learn now.

Even with these caveats, the chance is clearly at hand to capitalize on community and citizen readiness for more responsibility.

In chapter 4, I mentioned "The Civic Index" of the National Civic League as an important tool to help communities evaluate and develop their civic capacity. A different look at successful communities was provided in a special edition of *National Civic Review* on "Civic Infrastructure." It deals with the question, "How is it that some communities can consistently confront and solve their problems while others cannot?"[27] I can't possibly do justice to this valuable document and its many experienced participants, but I can pass along many of the major points as summarized by the editor, David Lampé, who begins: "In successful community after successful community, there is a recurring pattern of civic engagement and broad commitment to values of openness, equality and mutual respect—in short, a style of conducting business embodied in what the National Civic League calls 'civic infrastructure.'" A summary of Lampé's list, drawn from the various authors, includes these pointers:

- Recognition that serious problems exist.
- Periodic renegotiation of the social contract between government, individuals, and private institutions.
- A well developed sense of personal responsibility for community success among citizens.
- Investment in "social capital," Putnam's "networks and norms of trust, reciprocity, and civic engagement."
- Community leaders who empower or at least provide an enabling role for their constituents and who can "navigate through diverse cultures, traditions, and interests."
- Returning a sense of responsibility, opportunity, and hope to neighborhoods and communities.
- Recognition that major problems can rarely be "solved by any single jurisdiction." The layers of government and others who must be involved "will require the development of *regional* civic infrastructure and regional citizenship."
- The "shared power nature of contemporary governance . . . [including] sharing resources, power, and information."[28]

A still different way of looking at what it takes to turn things around is provided by columnist Neal R. Peirce in "The Case for an American Renewal," from another issue of *National Civic Review*. Peirce obviously knows the lists provided by others, but adds such bedrock considerations as passion, energy, exhilaration, patriotism, courage, and pride. For example:

A recent Teacher of the Year in Illinois discarded everything that impeded achievement in the classroom—the rules, the bureaucrats, even the textbooks. She couldn't change the poverty of the neighborhood, but she changed the values of the students, with startling results. . . .

[A] renewal must also be filled with exhilaration and potential—a sense of possibility for our lives and a society from which we draw more fulfillment and can take infinitely more pride.

Fundamentally, the message of *American Renewal* is that we need a new patriotism—as bold as the raw courage of the nation's founders, as visionary as the framers of the most durable democracy in recorded history—because we face the challenge of reorganizing some of our most complex and resistant systems.[29]

I mentioned in chapter 4 some sources for examples of successes in specific areas of governance such as schools, transportation, and criminal justice. Among the best of these are: The Program for Community Problem Solving of the International City/County Management Association (ICMA), a database of innovative programs that have worked and which have been written up for use by other communities, and the Civic Engagement Network, which often operates in cooperation with ICMA to publicize the success stories through telecommunication such as the Internet.

One of the reasons so many examples in community problem solving are so little known and used is that as a nation we are absolutely terrible at replication. We tend to insist that "our community is different" or we hold to the parochial pride of "not invented here." Also, we are not very good at creating the partnerships necessary to deal with almost all of the complex, intertwined problems facing us. We need to convince and train people to learn, adapt, and apply solutions found elsewhere and to build the collaborations necessary for success in their communities.

7. Build on the country's already pervasive independent
sector to achieve greater participation and impact—
without exaggerating what voluntary organizations
can do or what government need not do.

The independent sector's advocacy and empowering roles are major ways by which voluntary and philanthropic organizations help democratize our country; and the sector's service organizations, such as nonprofit universities, hospitals, and museums are the envy of the world. Together, these contributions represent a large force for the empowering of Americans.

The associations and institutions of the independent sector should not be viewed nor should they view themselves as essentially adversarial to government. Their far larger function is to strengthen civil society, including democratic government.

It is essential to maintain the sector's relative independence from undue governmental control. Nothing in this denies the government's absolutely appropriate responsibility to be certain that voluntary organizations are worthy of the special privileges provided by tax exemption, but within that expectation, the organizations of the sector should be as free as possible to provide the alternatives, experimentation, and criticism for which society most depends on them.

Nothing in the roles and record's of nonprofit organizations should obscure their continuing and growing responsibility to prove themselves legitimate, responsive, effective, and accountable. As underscored in INDEPENDENT SECTOR's report "Ethics and the Nation's Voluntary and Philanthropic Community," "Those who presume to serve the public good assume a public trust."[30]

We may be at a point in our civic life to return to something like the civic leagues that existed in so many communities in the early twentieth century. They played a pivotal role in strengthening governance, including citizen involvement and influence. Their resurgence should be encouraged.

We should also encourage foundations and corporate social responsibility programs, which are among the nation's few sources of independent social capital for nonprofit endeavor and civic investing. That includes allowing foundations to exist at least for the long term, not setting time constraints on how long foundations may exist. When I compare all the good arguments against perpetual trusts (the foundation's purpose loses relevance; the staff becomes so professional that the original purposes are suffocated; the foundation is controlled by a "dead hand") with the relatively few foundation dollars there are—certainly compared to government expenditures—I come down on the side of longevity. I have repeatedly come across the enormous current impact of such foundations as Ford, Carnegie, Rockefeller, Commonwealth, and Kellogg. Had they all gone the way of Rosenwald, Fleischmann, Hubert, and Whitney, I wonder if there would be nearly the positive influence of this "extra dimension" on society today.

In terms of the priority of civic investing, Susan V. Berresford, head of the Ford Foundation, says: "The first challenge is the uncertainty people express about their ability to create change in the face of seemingly negative and powerful forces. Foundations can respond by helping to project the visions of inspirational individuals involved in the struggle to improve human well being."[31]

Although we must not exaggerate the worth of philanthropic effort, particularly if it obscures our responsibility to democratic government, we must also not underestimate how much this participation means to our opportunities to be unique and free as individuals and as a society. Through our voluntary initiative and independent institutions, ever more Americans worship freely, study quietly, are cared for compassionately, experiment creatively, serve effectively, advocate aggressively, and contribute generously. These national characteristics are constantly beautiful and must remain beautifully constant.

8. Establish regular evaluations of the state of our democracy with careful attention to civil society.

At least once each decade we should evaluate the state of our democracy, including civil society and its various components. This will provide a fairly specific way to determine if democracy itself is strong and whether its underpinnings need strengthening.

In late 1998, the National Commission on Civic Renewal issued its final report which included a central recommendation for an "Index of National Civic Health" and its regular use "to improve our civic condition."[32]

We regularly assess the state of our economy, education test scores, the census, and various other aspects of our national condition. Why not the most important consideration, the state of our democracy? It is, after all, the basis on which this free nation was established and on which all else depends.

9. Develop a large and sustained effort to promote civility as the most elemental expectation of American citizenship.

In *The Idea of Civil Society*, Seligman lays out the wondrous possibilities of civil society, but ends with this plea for at least minimal aspiration: "no loss of hope is the contribution we can make to the future establishment of, if not civil *society*, then at least a more civil one."[33]

8

Summing Up:
Prospects for an Enduring Democracy

This is my letter to the World.
EMILY DICKINSON

Through all my hopefulness, I must still confront the awful question of whether this democracy will survive another century and maybe beyond. No other democracy has lasted as long as ours, so we cannot assume that ours will just keep rolling on.

My sense is that the prospects are reasonably good. The design of our government, including the power of citizens to shape it, is still essentially intact. Our problems in the last part of the twentieth century are not nearly as great as the traumas of the second half of the preceding one, and our progress in protecting and extending democracy for most Americans has been dramatic. We also have a fairly clear grasp of what we can do to preserve and strengthen civil society and therefore democracy. With common sense and some luck, we should be all right.

But despite my general optimism I worry, and most of what I worry about is whether 250 years beyond our founding it is really practical to expect that people will realize that it could still come apart and whether they will do everything possible to keep that from happening.

Though it seems eminently logical that rational people would never ever let such a democracy unravel, I've been around long enough and read enough to know that people and history can be tragically irrational.

I find myself worrying what the consequences would be if in the course of the new century we experience a worsening of such factors as selfishness, taking liberty for granted, governmental limits on citizen participation, the influence of special interests on public officials, separation between the haves and have-nots, intolerance, and incivility. How much deterioration of our civil society would it take to weaken democracy irreparably?

Gibbon's observations on the decline of Athenian democracy keep ringing in my ears, so I repeat them here:

> In the end, more than they wanted freedom, they wanted security. They wanted a comfortable life and they lost it all—security, comfort and freedom. . . . When the Athenians finally wanted not to give to society but for society to give to them, when the freedom they wished for most was freedom from responsibility, then Athens ceased to be free.[1]

Perhaps I've already said everything I can about our privileges and responsibilities, but I come to the end of the book with a sense of inadequacy. I don't feel I've really fulfilled my obligation to pass along the essence of what a privileged lifetime within civil society has taught me.

For fifty years, coinciding with the last half of the extraordinary twentieth century, I have been in the midst of citizen movements dealing with some of the most urgent causes of these times, and along the way have learned what it really means for people to be liberated and what is required to maintain the enabling and ennobling freedoms.

When I match the meaning of those lessons against what I consider to be the public's limited grasp of them and against my firsthand awareness of how easily our rights as empowered citizens are eroded, I feel I should go on and on with writing and explaining and exclaiming.

I realize of course that more of the same won't help and would only limit my chances to reach my audience of *public intellectuals* who might be willing to be informed but not inundated. At the risk of overstepping that boundary slightly, I cling to this chance for what the French elegantly call the "envoi," or parting word, so that

I might try at least to end my message with energy and urgency. There are five points I want to leave with you, quite literally:

1. How essential civil society is to a civilized existence and to a fully functioning democracy.
2. That as important as civil society is, it is largely invisible.
3. Even America's seemingly vibrant civil society is fragile and easily subject to attack and neglect, both of which undermine our freedoms.
4. The greatest dangers to civil society and democracy arise from neglect by the very citizens who expect privileges and rights without exercising responsibility to protect them.
5. People throughout the world envy and strive for our degree of civil society and effective democracy, but here in our privileged setting we don't know what we've got or how much it takes to hold onto it.

To inspire an abiding awareness of each of these points, I want somehow to press on until every citizen pledges to Alexander Hamilton's "vow of eternal vigilance."

Far short of that, I have to accept that this book must serve as "my letter to the World," to borrow Emily Dickinson's apt description of a heartfelt message aimed at everyone out there.[2] My "letter" to everyone is about the glory of our freedoms, coupled with our responsibility to pass them on to future generations.

The Indians who were quite literally the Native Americans believed in responsibility to the "seventh generation," meaning that every major act of communal life was to be measured for its impact on the seventh successor generation. Though that might exceed the reach of most of us, it should convey our responsibility to be as certain as possible that our civil society and democracy will provide liberating freedoms and opportunities for successive generations, including our great, great, great, great grandchildren.

For those who would respond that it's not practical to plan that far ahead or who believe that we can't know what major events, even calamities, could change everything between now and then, it is useful to consider how much we owe to those we commonly call our founding fathers, of whom we are little more than their seventh generation. Consider too that the freedoms they fought for are far less likely to be lost in an apocalypse than through our indifference or lack of will.

When such worries begin to make me grim, I realize that we at least have a choice about what kind of a nation we will be, and choosing to hold onto liberty is astronomically better than struggling to attain it in the first place.

Our democracy can last, but only if we accept and practice the enduring covenant recently and cogently summarized by John Gardner:

> Freedom and responsibility
> Liberty and duty
> That's the deal.[3]

For the sake of the seventh generation, I pray we will solemnly commit to that pledge and prepare our children and their children to pass it on.

Notes

1. Civil Society—Our Invisible Colossus (pp. 1–9)

1. CIVICUS, "Citizens: Strengthening Global Civil Society," Organization Committee Report (Washington, D.C.: CIVICUS, 1993), 3.
2. Ernest Gellner, *Conditions of Liberty: Civil Society and Its Rivals* (New York: Allan Lane/Penguin Press, 1994), 13.
3. Vaclav Havel in a speech given in Athens, May 24, 1993, on receiving the Onassis Prize for Man and Mankind.
4. Learned Hand, *Civitas: A Framework for Civic Education*, ed. Charles F. Bahmueller, John H. Buchanan, Jr., and Charles N. Quigley. National Council for the Social Studies Bulletin no. 86 (Calabasas, Calif.: Center for Civic Education, 1991), 12.
5. Thomas Jefferson, cited in *Kettering Review* (Winter 1994), 20.
6. Helen Ingram and Stephen Rathgeb Smith, *Public Policy for Democracy* (Washington, D.C.: Brookings Institution, 1993), 21.
7. Brian O'Connell, keynote address to the National Conference on Higher Education, Chicago (March 17, 1985), sponsored by American Association of Higher Education, Washington, D.C.
8. Robert L. Payton, *Philanthropy: Voluntary Action for the Public Good* (New York: W. W. Norton Company, 1987), 111.

2. Definitions and Descriptions (pp. 10–26)

1. Benjamin Barber, "Strengthening Democracy by Recreating Civil Society." For INDEPENDENT SECTOR Conference on Civil Society, Sept. 5, 1996, Washington, D.C.
2. Saul Alinsky, *Rules for Radicals: A Practical Primer for Realistic Radicals* (New York: Random House, 1971), xxv.
3. William F. Buckley, Jr., *Gratitude: Reflections on What We Owe to Our Country* (New York: Random House, 1990), 18.
4. Sara M. Evans and Harry C. Boyte, *Free Spaces: The Sources of Democratic Change in America* (Chicago: University of Chicago Press, 1992), viii.
5. Ibid., 17.
6. Ann Morrow Lindbergh, *Gift From the Sea* (New York: Pantheon Books, 1955), 128.

7. John W. Gardner, *Building Community* (Washington, D.C.: INDE-PENDENT SECTOR, 1991), 5.

8. Webster's *New Universal Unabridged Dictionary*, 2d ed. (1979), s.v. "civility."

9. James A. Joseph, "On Moral Imperatives," *Foundation News*, 36, no. 6 (November/December 1995), 10.

10. Robert Putnam, "The Prosperous Community: Social Capital and Public Life," *The American Prospect*, no. 13 (Spring 1993), 2.

3. Origins of Our Extraordinary Civil Society (pp. 27–38)

1. Brian O'Connell, "Our Religious Heritage," in *America's Voluntary Spirit* (New York: Foundation Center, 1983), 1.

2. Robert Bremner, *American Philanthropy* (Chicago: University of Chicago Press, 1988), 5.

3. John Winthrop, "A Model of Christian Charity," cited in *America's Voluntary Spirit*, ed. Brian O'Connell (New York: Foundation Center, 1983), 29–33.

4. Max Lerner, "The Joiners," in *America's Voluntary Spirit*, ed. Brian O'Connell (New York: Foundation Center, 1983), 81.

5. Richard W. Lyman, "What Kind of Society Shall We Have?" occasional paper (Washington, D.C.: INDEPENDENT SECTOR, 1981).

6. Thomas Jefferson, cited in *Civitas: A Framework for Civic Education*, ed. Charles F. Bahmueller, John H. Buchanan, Jr., and Charles N. Quigley. National Council for the Social Studies Bulletin no. 86 (Calabasas, Calif.: Center for Civic Education, 1991), 637.

7. Lech Walesa, "200th Anniversary of the Bill of Rights," Philip Morris Companies and the National Archives (Washington, D.C.: 1990).

8. Based on conversations with constitutional scholar Adam Yarmolinsky, and a summary letter from him dated February 2, 1998.

9. CIVICUS, *Legal Principles for Citizen Participation: Toward a Legal Framework for Civil Society Organizations*, (Washington, D.C.: CIVICUS, 1997).

10. Virginia A. Hodgkinson, Paul G. Schervish, and Margaret Gates, eds., "Caring, Involvement and Community," in *Care and Community in Modern Society: Passing on the Tradition of Service to Future Generations* (San Francisco: Jossey-Bass Publishers, 1995), 46.

11. Estelle James, research in progress. With her assumption of responsibilities at The World Bank, the final stages of this research were temporarily suspended. However, it is far enough along for her to believe that these findings are valid. Dr. James affirmed this in a letter to me dated October 18, 1997. Preliminary and related findings were reported

in *The Nonprofit Sector in International Perspective: Studies in Cooperative Cultures and Policy* (New York: Oxford University Press, 1989), 3–27.

12. William M. Sullivan, "The Infrastructure of Democracy,"in *Democracy Is a Discussion: Civic Engagement in Emerging Democracies*, ed. Sondra Myers (New London Conn.: Connecticut College, 1996), 11. (This is a discussion by Sullivan of Robert Putnam's *Making Democracy Work: Civic Traditions in Modern Italy* [Princeton, N.J.: Princeton University Press, 1993], 87–90.)

13. James Luther Adams, *Voluntary Associations: Socio-Cultural Analyses and Theological Interpretation*, ed. J. Ronald Engel (Chicago: Exploration Press, 1986), 235.

14. David Mathews, "The Constitution and the Independent Sector," keynote address to the Research Forum, INDEPENDENT SECTOR, Washington, D.C., 1987.

15. Peter Dobkin Hall, "Private Philanthropy and Public Policy: A Historical Appraisal," in *Philanthropy: Four Views* (New Brunswick, N.J.: Transaction Books, 1988), 46–47.

16. Sidney Verba, Kay Lehman Schlozman, and Henry E. Brady, *Voice and Equality: Civic Voluntarism in American Politics* (Cambridge, Mass.: Harvard University Press, 1995), 528–29.

17. Adam B. Seligman, "Civil Society, Citizenship and the Representation of Society," in *The Idea of Civil Society* (Princeton, N.J.: Princeton University Press, 1992), 103.

18. Ibid., 109.

19. Alexis de Tocqueville, "Of the Uses Which Americans Make of Public Associations in Civil Life," in *Democracy in America*, vol. 2 (New York: Alfred A. Knopf, Borzoi Books, 1976), 106.

20. Richard Reeves, *American Journey* (New York: Simon and Schuster, 1982), 13.

21. Gordon S. Wood, "Thomas Jefferson, Equality and the Creation of a Civil Society," *Fordham Law Review*, 64, no. 5 (April 1996), 2133–47.

22. Ibid.

23. Jean Bethke Elshtain, *Democracy on Trial* (New York: Basic Books, 1995), 35–36.

4. Effective Citizenship → Effective Government → Effective Citizenship (pp. 39–55)

1. Center for Civic Education, *Civitas: A Framework for Civic Education*, National Council for the Social Studies Bulletin no. 86, ed. Charles F. Bahmueller, John H. Buchanan, Jr., and Charles N. Quigley (Calabasas, Calif.: Center for Civic Education, 1991), 3.

2. From the Athenian Code. This section of the code decorates the foyer of the Maxwell Graduate School of Citizenship and Public Affairs, Syracuse University, Syracuse, New York.

3. Edward Gibbon, cited in "The Moral Foundations of Society" by Margaret Thatcher, for the Website "The Ultimate Truth," *Conservative Consensus* (Seattle, Wash., 1995), 2.

4. Theodore Roosevelt. From the *Washington Post* "For The Record" column of November 2, 1982, citing recent remarks by Edith Roosevelt Derby Williams, granddaughter of Theodore Roosevelt, at Arlington Cemetery.

5. Michael Pertschuk, *Giant Killers* (New York: W. W. Norton Company, 1987), 12.

6. Frances Moore Lappé and Paul Martin DuBois, *The Quickening of America: Rebuilding Our Nation, Remaking Our Lives* (San Francisco, Jossey-Bass Publishers, 1994), 165.

7. Jeffrey M. Berry, Kent E. Portney, and Ken Thomson, *The Rebirth of Urban Democracy* (Washington, D.C.: Brookings Institution, 1993), 294.

8. Eugene W. Hickok, "Federalism, Citizenship and Community," from the newsletter of the Civil Society Project, vol. 3, no. 1 (May 1996), 1–8.

9. David Mathews, "The Public in Practice and Theory," *Public Administration Review*, 44, special issue (March 1984) 120–25. (Adapted from a lecture for the Maxwell School of Citizenship and Public Affairs, Syracuse University, Syracuse, New York, June 30, 1983.)

10. Bruce Sievers, "Can Philanthropy Solve the Problems of Civil Society?" a report of the inaugural meeting of the International Conference on Civil Society (San Juan, P.R., January 31–February 4, 1994).

11. Peter L. Berger and Richard John Neuhaus, "To Empower People: The Role of Mediating Structures in Public Policy" (Washington, D.C.: American Enterprise Institute for Public Policy Research, 1977).

12. David Mathews, *Is There a Public for Public Schools* (Dayton, Ohio: Kettering Foundation Press, 1996), 8.

13. Daniel Boorstin, "Democracy's Secret Virtue," *Kettering Review* (Winter 1994), 16.

14. John Clark, "The State, Popular Participation and the Voluntary Sector," *World Development*, 23, no. 4 (1995), 593–601.

15. Brian O'Connell, *Philanthropy in Action* (New York: Foundation Center, 1987), 91.

16. Luther Gulick, *National Institute of Public Administration: A Progress Report* (New York: National Institute of Public Administration, 1928).

17. Jane S. Dahlberg, *The New York Bureau of Municipal Research: Pioneer in Government Administration* (New York: New York University Press, 1966).

18. Ibid., 62.

19. Frederick C. Mosher, "Public Administration," *Encyclopedia Britannica*, 15th ed.; 1974.

20. Ralph R. Widner, "Citizen and Public Administrator: Rearranging the Connection," 1997, paper given at spring meeting, National Academy of Public Administration, Duke University (Durham, N.C., June 6–8), 1.

21. Ibid.

22. Brian O'Connell, "Future Leadership in America," in *People Power: Service, Advocacy, Empowerment* (New York: Foundation Center, 1994), 181.

23. Harlan Cleveland, in an address to Common Cause on its tenth anniversary (Washington, D.C., 1980).

24. David Broder, *Changing of the Guard: Power and Leadership in America* (New York: Simon & Schuster, 1980).

25. Henry Steele Commager, *Commager on Tocqueville* (Columbia, Mo.: University of Missouri Press, 1993), ix.

26. James A. Morone, *The Democratic Wish: Popular Participation and the Limits of American Government* (New York: Collier Macmillan Publishers, 1988), 322.

27. John W. Gardner, *National Renewal* (Washington, D.C.: INDEPENDENT SECTOR and the National Civic League, September 1995).

28. Nancy Kruh, "Across the United States, Citizens Are Discovering the Key to the Country's Social Problems Is Within Themselves," *Dallas Morning News*, July 29, 1996.

29. Brian O'Connell, *Powered by Coalition: The Story of* INDEPENDENT SECTOR (San Francisco, Calif.: Jossey-Bass Publishers, 1997), 157.

30. National Civic League, "Tales of Turnaround" 82, no. 4 (Fall 1993).

31. National Civic League, "Civic Index" (Denver, Colo. National Civic League, 1993).

32. Richard Goodwin, column on campaign finance reform in the *Boston Globe*, February 5, 1997.

5. Volunteers, Voluntary Organizations, and Private Philanthropy: The Independent Sector (pp. 56–75)

1. Virginia A. Hodgkinson and Murray Weitzman, *Giving and Volunteering in the United States* (Washington, D.C.: INDEPENDENT SECTOR, 1996).

2. Nathan Hale, credo of the Lend A Hand Society, Philadelphia, 1885.

3. Merle Curti, "American Philanthropy and the National Character," *American Quarterly* 10, no. 4 (Winter 1958): 420–37.

4. Brian O'Connell, *America's Voluntary Spirit: A Book of Readings* (New York: Foundation Center, 1983), 227.

5. INDEPENDENT SECTOR, National Taxonomy of Exempt Entities (Washington, D.C.: INDEPENDENT SECTOR, 1987).

6. Brian O'Connell, *People Power: Service, Advocacy, Empowerment* (New York: Foundation Center, 1994).

7. Sara M. Evans and Harry C. Boyte, *Free Spaces: The Sources of Democratic Change in America* (Chicago: University of Chicago Press, 1992), xiii.

8. Helen Ingram and Stephen Rathgeb Smith, *Public Policy for Democracy* (Washington, D.C.: Brookings Institution, 1993), 239.

9. Robert Wuthnow, *Sharing the Journey: Support Groups and America's New Quest for Community* (New York: The Free Press, 1994), 12.

10. Ibid.

11. Jeffrey M. Berry, Kent E. Portney, and Ken Thomson, *The Rebirth of Urban Democracy* (Washington D.C.: Brookings Institution, 1993), 290.

12. James Luther Adams, *Voluntary Associations: Socio-Cultural Analyses and Theological Interpretation*, ed. J. Ronald Engel (Chicago: Exploration Press, 1986), 242.

13. Franklin I. Gamwell, *Beyond Preference: Liberal Theories of Independent Associations* (Chicago: University of Chicago Press, 1984), 154.

14. John W. Gardner, in *America's Voluntary Spirit*, ed. Brian O'Connell (New York: Foundation Center, 1983), xiii.

15. Brian O'Connell, remarks at the charter meeting of INDEPENDENT SECTOR (Washington, D.C., March 5, 1980).

16. Saul Alinsky, *Rules for Radicals: A Practical Primer for Realistic Radicals* (New York: Random House, 1971), 113.

17. Brian O'Connell, *Voices from the Heart: In Celebration of America's Volunteers* (San Francisco: Chronicle Books and Jossey-Bass Publishers, 1999), 50.

18. Peter L. Berger and Richard John Neuhaus, *To Empower People: The Role of Mediating Structures in Public Policy* (Washington, D.C.: American Enterprise Institute for Public Policy Research, 1977).

19. Sidney Verba, Kay Lehman Schlozman, and Henry E. Brady, *Voice and Equality: Civic Voluntarism in American Politics* (Cambridge, Mass.: Harvard University Press, 1995), 18.

20. Brian O'Connell, *Philanthropy in Action* (New York: Foundation Center, 1987), 3.

21. Ibid., 13–14 (from Milton Lomask's *Seed Money: The Guggenheim Story* [New York: Farrar Straus and Co., 1964]).

22. Ibid., 31–32 (from the official history of Stanford University).

23. Ibid., 45 (from Henry Allen Moe's Founders' Day address at Johns Hopkins University, 1951).

24. Ibid., 47 (from Arthur Davis Wright's "The Negro Rural School Fund" in *The Anna T. Jeanes Foundation, 1907–1933*, [Washington, D.C.: 1933]).

25. Ibid., 118.

26. Ibid., 151–52 (from William G. Roger's *Ladies Bountiful*, [New York: Harcourt, Brace and World, 1968]).

27. Ibid., 51–52 (from Arnaud C. Marts' *Philanthropy's Role in Civilization: Its Contribution to Human Freedom* [New York: Harper & Bros., 1973]).

28. Ibid.

29. Alex Plinio and Joanne Scanlon, *Resource Raising: The Role of Non-Cash Assistance in Corporate Philanthropy* (Washington, D.C.: INDEPENDENT SECTOR, 1986).

30. Brian O'Connell, *Philanthropy in Action*, 210–11.

31. F. Emerson Andrews, *Corporation Philanthropy* (New York: Russell Sage Foundation, 1953), 23–28.

32. INDEPENDENT SECTOR, *Corporate Philanthropy*, 7, no. 4 (August/September 1987), Washington, D.C.

33. Philip E. Mosely, "International Affairs," in *U.S. Philanthropic Foundations: Their History, Structure, Management, and Record*, ed. Warren Weaver (New York: Harper & Row, 1967), 375.

34. Brian O'Connell, *Philanthropy in Action*, 273.

6. Limitations of Civil Society, Threats to It, and the General State of It (pp. 76–105)

1. Virginia A. Hodgkinson, Murray S. Weitzman, et al. *Nonprofit Almanac: 1996–1997* (San Francisco: Jossey-Bass Publishers; and Washington, D.C.: INDEPENDENT SECTOR, 1996), 2–4.

2. Brian O'Connell, *People Power: Service, Advocacy, Empowerment* (New York: Foundation Center, 1994), 104.

3. Sara M. Evans and Harry C. Boyte, *Free Spaces: The Sources of Democratic Change in America* (Chicago, Ill.: University of Chicago Press, 1992), 19.

4. Ibid., 15.

5. Sidney Verba, Kay Lehman Schlozman, and Henry E. Brady, *Voice and Equality: Civic Voluntarism in American Politics* (Cambridge, Mass.: Harvard University Press, 1995), 532–33.

6. Jeffrey M. Berry, Kent E. Portney, and Ken Thomson, *The Rebirth of Urban Democracy* (Washington, D.C.: Brookings Institution, 1993), 299.

7. Virginia A. Hodgkinson, "Key Challenges Facing the Nonprofit Sector," in *The Future of the Nonprofit Sector: Challenges, Changes, and Policy Considerations*, ed. Virginia A. Hodgkinson, Richard W. Lyman, and Associates (San Francisco, Calif.: Jossey-Bass Publishers; and Washington, D.C.: INDEPENDENT SECTOR, 1989), 18.

8. Edmund Burke, cited in *Civitas: A Framework for Civic Education*, ed. Charles F. Bahmueller, John H. Buchanan, Jr., and Charles N. Quigley. National Council for the Social Studies Bulletin no. 86 (Calabasas, Calif.: Center for Civic Education, 1991), 628.

9. Brian O'Connell, "The Relationship Between Voluntary Organizations and Government: Constructive Partnerships/Creative Tensions," speech given to the National Academy of Public Administration (Washington, D.C., June 5, 1986).

10. Brian O'Connell, "What Voluntary Activity Can and Cannot Do for America," *Public Administration Review* (September/October 1989), 486–91.

11. Brian O'Connell, *Powered by Coalition: The Story of INDEPENDENT SECTOR* (San Francisco, Calif.: Jossey-Bass Publishers, 1997), 63–64.

12. Brian O'Connell, "Don't Save Me from the Left or Right," *Christian Science Monitor*, December 28, 1983.

13. Frederick Douglass, escaped slave, abolitionist, and first black to hold high office in the federal government, probably wrote these lines for his paper, *North Star*. A colleague sent them to me to feature in one of my New Year's cards, which I did in 1977. Recently, two other admirers of Douglass assured me that they are his words but they too do not know the specific source. If a reader does, I would like to add it to any subsequent edition.

14. John Harlan, Supreme Court justice, writing for the Court in *Cohen v. California*, as reported by Nat Hentoff in "First Amendment Roarers," *Washington Post*, January 17, 1987.

15. O'Connell, *Powered by Coalition*, 84.

16. Ibid.

17. Ibid., 103.

18. James Luther Adams, *Voluntary Associations: Socio-Cultural Analyses and Theological Interpretations* (Chicago, Ill.: Exploration Press, 1986), 217.

19. Henry Owen, "Remembering the Days of the Holocaust," *Washington Post*, April 27, 1996.

20. Francis Fukuyama, in a review of Ernest Gellner's *Conditions of Liberty*, *Times Literary Supplement*, October 28, 1994.

21. Stephen C. Craig, *The Malevolent Leaders: Popular Discontent in America* (Boulder, Colo.: Westview Press, Inc., 1993), 184.

22. Georgie Anne Geyer, *Americans No More: The Death of Citizenship* (New York: Atlantic Monthly Press, 1996), book jacket.

23. Daniel Yankelovich, *Kettering Review* (Fall 1995), 6.

24. Robert D. Putnam, "Tuning In, Tuning Out: The Strange Disap-

pearance of Social Capital in America," *Political Science and Politics*, 28, no. 4 (December 1995), 667–80.

25. Yankelovich, *Kettering Review*, 15.

26. David Broder, "Poll Dispels Notion of 'Civic Slugs,' " *Daily Oklahoman*, December 17, 1997.

27. Alan Wolfe, *One Nation, After All* (New York: Viking, 1998), 154–55.

28. Everett C. Ladd, "A Vast Empirical Record Refutes the Idea of Civic Decline," *The Public Perspective* 7, no. 4 (June/July 1996).

29. Robert J. Samuelson, " 'Bowling Alone' Is Bunk," *Washington Post*, October 4, 1996.

30. Charles Stewart Mott Foundation, "America's Tattered Tapestry: Can We Reclaim Our Civility through Connectedness?" annual report (Flint, Mich.: Charles Stewart Mott Foundation, 1995), 18.

31. John W. Gardner, *National Renewal* (Washington, D.C.: INDEPENDENT SECTOR and National Civic League, September 1995), 5.

32. National Civic League, "America's Cities and Communities: Problems and People Power" (Princeton, N.J.: George Gallup International Institute, November 1990).

33. The Harwood Group, "Citizens and Politics: A View from Main Street America," report prepared for the Kettering Foundation (June 1991).

34. Joseph S. Nye, Jr., "Introduction: The Decline of Confidence in Government," in *Why People Don't Trust Government*, ed. Joseph S. Nye, Jr., Philip D. Zelikow, and David C. King (Cambridge, Mass.: Harvard University Press, 1997), 1.

35. Ibid., 3.

36. U.S. Department of Commerce, *Statistical Abstract of the United States, 1997: The National Data Book* (Washington, D.C.: U.S. Department of Commerce, October 1997), 288.

37. The New World Foundation, "Democracy in America: Towards Greater Participation" (New York: The New World Foundation, 1982).

38. Ibid.

39. National Civic League, "America's Cities and Communities."

40. The Harwood Group, "Citizens and Politics."

41. Helen Ingram and Steven Rathgeb Smith, eds., *Public Policy for Democracy* (Washington, D.C.: Brookings Institution, 1993), 12.

42. Benjamin R. Barber, "Public Space for a Civil Society in Eclipse," *Kettering Review* (Fall 1995), 12.

43. Derek Bok, "Measuring the Performance of Government," in *Why People Don't Trust Government*, ed. Joseph S. Nye, Jr., Philip Zelikow, and

David C. King (Cambridge, Mass.: Harvard University Press, 1997), 56.

44. Ibid., 61.

45. Michael Sviridoff, "The Seeds of Urban Renewal," *The Public Interest* (Winter 1994).

46. Alex Comfort, *The Song of Lazarus* (New York: Viking Press, 1945), 93.

47. John W. Gardner, "Building Community" (Washington, D.C.: INDEPENDENT SECTOR, 1991), 15.

48. John W. Gardner, "National Renewal" (Washington, D.C.: INDEPENDENT SECTOR and The National Civic League, 1995), 24–25.

7. Preserving and Strengthening Civil Society (pp. 106–122)

1. Jean Bethke Elshtain, "The Politics of Displacement," in *Democracy on Trial* (New York: Basic Books, 1995), 37–38.

2. R. Freeman Butts, introduction to *Civitas: A Framework for Civic Education*, ed. Charles F. Bahmueller, John H. Buchanan, Jr., and Charles N. Quigley. National Council for the Social Studies Bulletin no. 86 (Calabasas, Calif.: Center for Civic Education, 1991), 1.

3. David Mathews, foreword to *Higher Education and the Practice of Democratic Politics: A Political Education Reader*, ed. Bernard Murchland (Dayton, Ohio: Kettering Foundation, 1991), xvi.

4. From the mission statement of Campus Compact (Providence, R.I.: Campus Compact, 1985).

5. Julie Bartsch and Patricia Barnicle, "Community Service Learning: A Successful Formula for School Change," the Lincoln Filene Center Report (Medford, Mass.: Tufts University, 1997), 1.

6. Vincent Harding, *Hope and History: Why We Must Share the Story of the Movement* (Maryknoll, N.Y.: Orbis Books, 1990), 180.

7. David Mathews, "The Public in Practice and Theory," *Public Administration Review*, special issue (March 1984), 120. (Adapted from a lecture for the Maxwell School of Citizenship and Public Affairs, Syracuse University, Syracuse, New York, June 30, 1983.)

8. Walter B. Wriston, "Bits, Bytes, and Diplomacy," *Foreign Affairs*, 76, no. 5 (September/October, 1997), 172.

9. Lawrence K. Grossman, *The Electronic Public: Reshaping Democracy in the Information Age* (New York: Penguin Books, 1995), 210.

10. Lawrence K. Grossman, "Technology Governance: A Public Interest Vision for the Telecommunications Age," Webb Lecture given to the National Academy of Public Administration (Washington, D.C., November 14, 1997).

11. Robert D. Putnam, "Tuning In, Tuning Out: The Strange Disap-

pearance of Social Capital in America," *Political Science and Politics*, 28, no. 4 (December 1995), 667–80.

12. Wriston, "Bits, Bytes and Diplomacy," 162.

13. Mark Jurkowitz, "Talking Back," *Boston Globe Magazine*, February 25, 1996, 15.

14. Ibid.

15. Harding, *Hope and History*, 12.

16. Ralph Waldo Emerson, cited in *Ralph Waldo Emerson*, by Frederick I. Carpenter (New York: American Book Company, 1934), 426.

17. *Care and Community in Modern Society: Passing on the Tradition of Service to Future Generations*, ed. Paul G. Schervish, Virginia A. Hodgkinson, Margaret Gates, and associates (San Francisco: Jossey-Bass Publishers/Washington, D.C.: INDEPENDENT SECTOR, 1995).

18. Ibid.

19. William S. White, in "America's Tattered Tapestry: Can We Reclaim Our Civility through Connectedness?" annual report (Flint Mich.: Charles Stewart Mott Foundation, 1995), 18.

20. Pam Solo, "Her Strategy for Civility: Start with Security," *Boston Sunday Globe*, December 15, 1996.

21. Robert L. Payton, *Philanthropy: Voluntary Action for the Public Good* (New York: Collier Macmillan Publishers/American Council on Education, 1988), 268.

22. David Mathews, "After Thoughts," *Kettering Review* (Winter 1994), 89.

23. Stephen C. Craig, *The Malevolent Leaders: Popular Discontent in America* (Boulder, Colo.: Westview Press, 1993), 180–83.

24. Harry C. Boyte, "Reinventing Citizenship," *Kettering Review* (Winter 1994), 87.

25. The Harwood Group, "Citizens and Politics: A View from Main Street America," report prepared for the Kettering Foundation (June 1991), 91.

26. Helen Ingram and Steven Rathgeb Smith, *Public Policy for Democracy* (Washington, D.C.: Brookings Institution, 1993), i.

27. David Lampé, "Civic Infrastructure," *National Civic Review*, 83, no. 2 (Spring 1993), 89.

28. Ibid., 90–92.

29. Neal R. Peirce, "The Case for an American Renewal," *National Civic Review*, 83, no. 1 (Winter/Spring 1994), 9.

30. INDEPENDENT SECTOR, "Ethics and the Nation's Voluntary and Philanthropic Community: Obedience to the Unenforceable" (Washington, D.C.: INDEPENDENT SECTOR, 1991).

31. Susan V. Berresford, "Challenges for Civil Society," an address to the City Club of Cleveland, Ohio (November 22, 1996).

32. "A Nation of Spectators: How Civic Engagement Weakens America and What We Can Do About It," The National Commission on Civic Renewal (College Park, Maryland, 1998), 24–32.

33. Adam B. Seligman, "Concluding Remarks on Civil Society," in *The Idea of Civil Society* (Princeton, N.J.: Princeton University Press, 1992), 206.

8. Summing Up: Prospects for an Enduring Democracy
(pp. 123–126)

1. Edward Gibbon, cited in "The Moral Foundations of Society" by Margaret Thatcher, for the Website "The Ultimate Truth," *Conservative Consensus* (Seattle, Wash., 1995), 2.

2. Emily Dickinson, *The Complete Poems of Emily Dickinson*, ed. Thomas H. Johnson (Boston: Little, Brown and Company, 1960), 211.

3. John W. Gardner, "Building Community" (Washington, D.C.: INDEPENDENT SECTOR, 1991), 10. Gardner's statement has appeared in slightly different variations. In a letter to me in summer 1998 he indicated that he prefers it as quoted on page 126.

Index